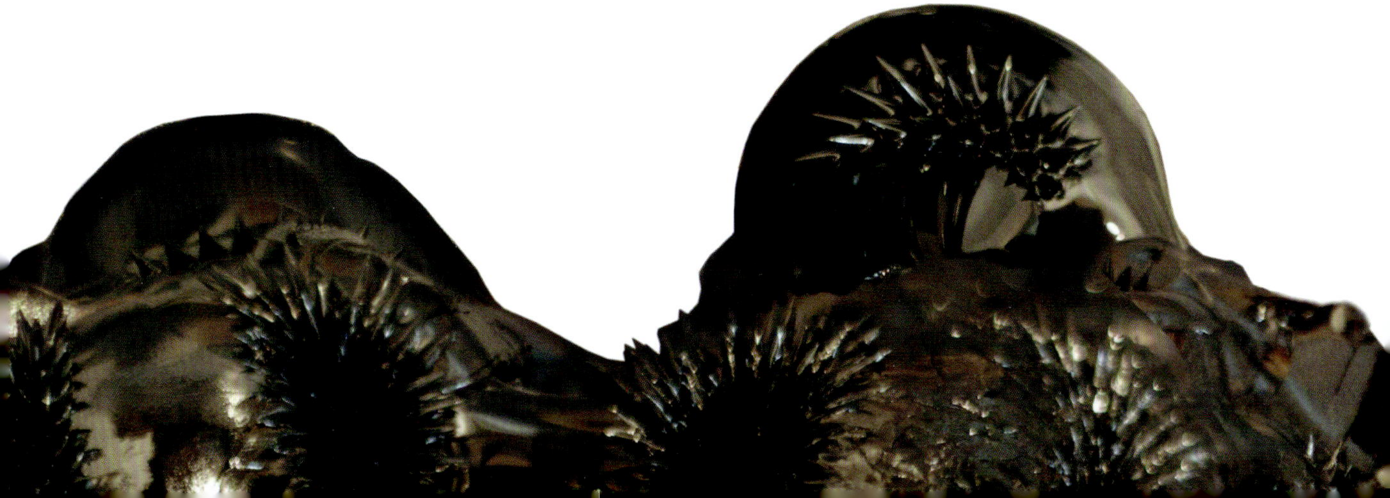

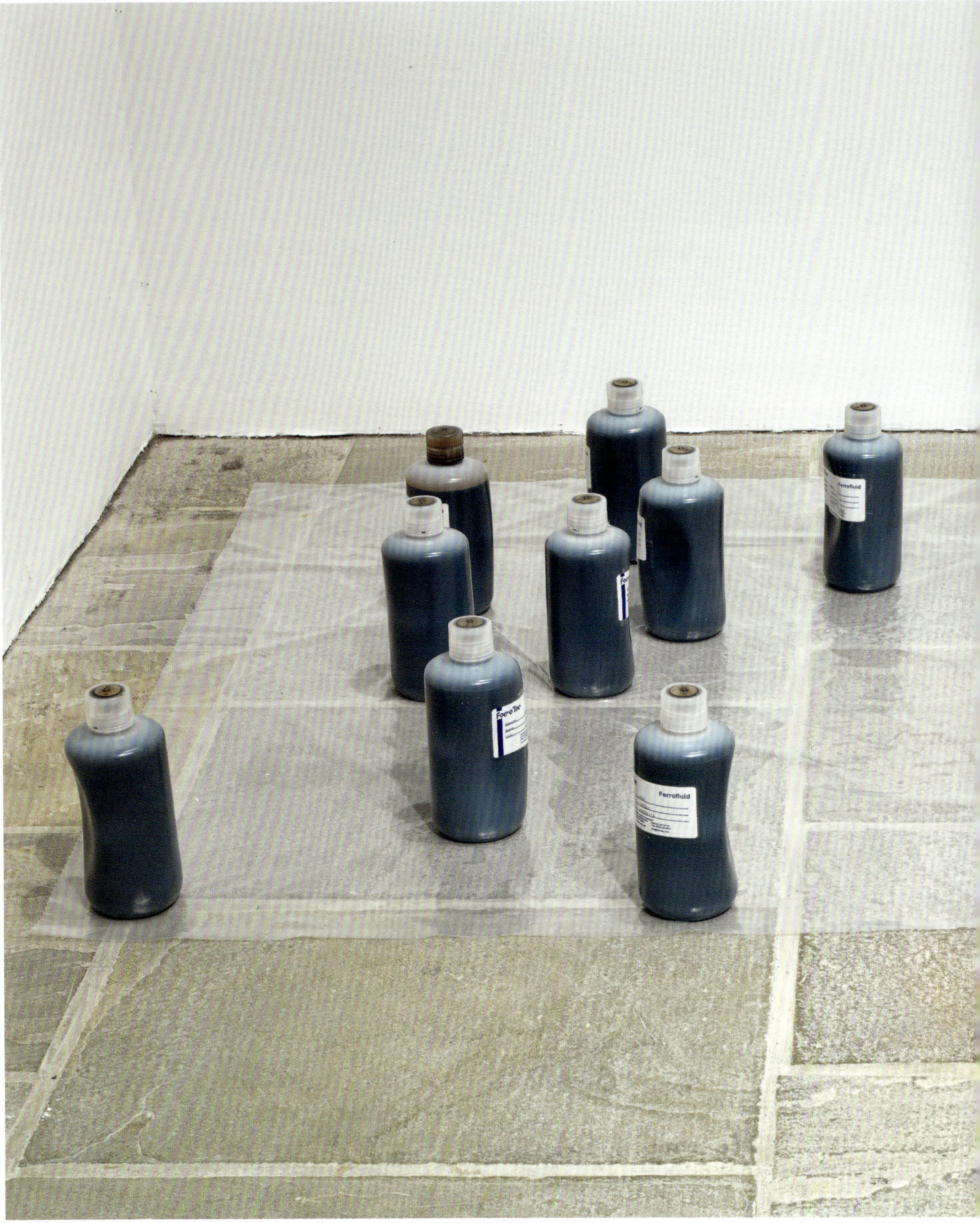
Ferrofluid
Ferrofluid

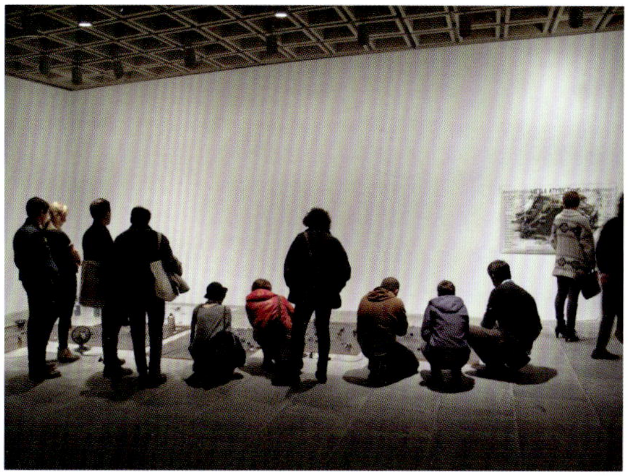

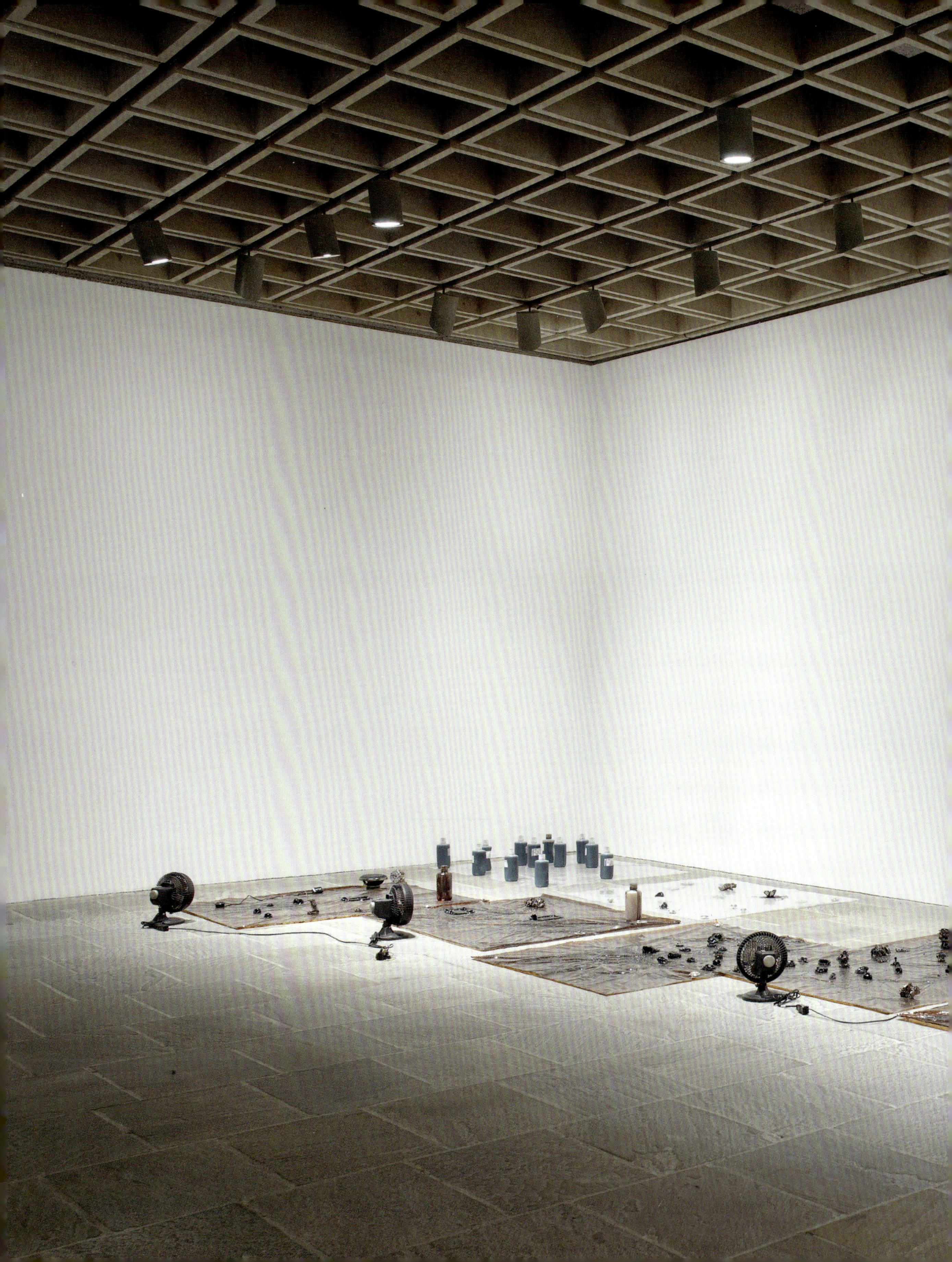

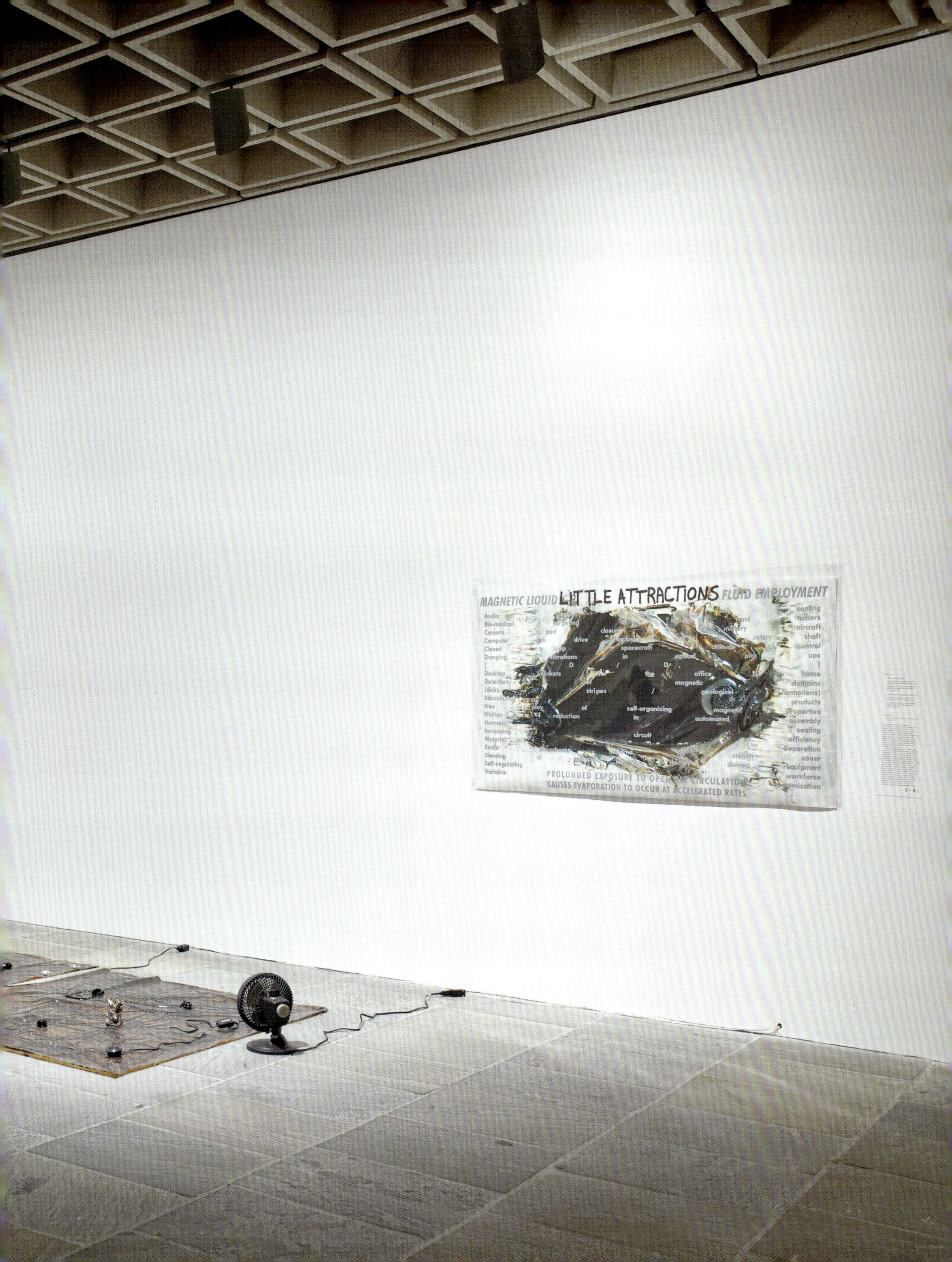
MAGNETIC LIQUID
LITTLE ATTRACTIONS
FLUID EMPLOYMENT
Audio
Bio-medical
Camera
Computer
Closed
Damping
Desktop
Detection
Free
Friction
Hermetic
Increasing
Material
Radar
Silencing
Self-regulating
Variable
cooling
tumors
aircraft
shaft
control
ups
home
domains
products
assembly
sealing
efficiency
Separation
cover
equipment
workforce
drive
spacecraft
optical
office
magnetic
stripes
self-organizing
automated
circuit
CAUSES EVAPORATION TO OCCUR AT ACCELERATED RATES

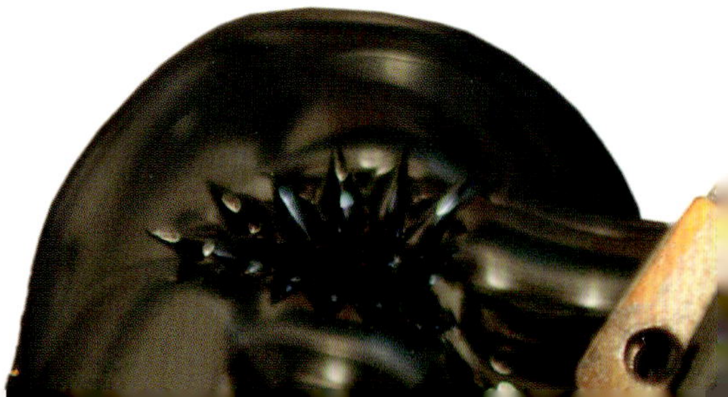

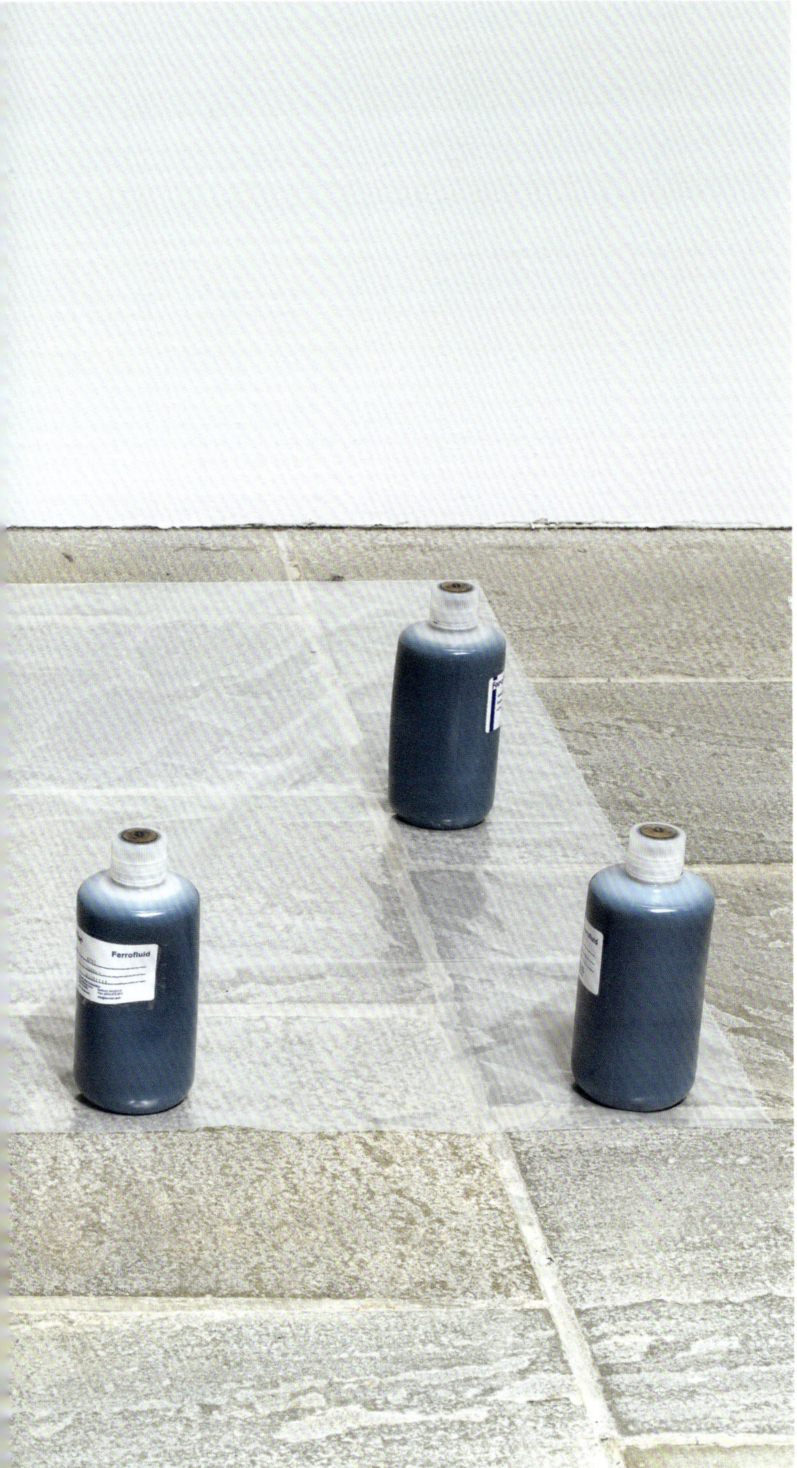
Ferrofluid

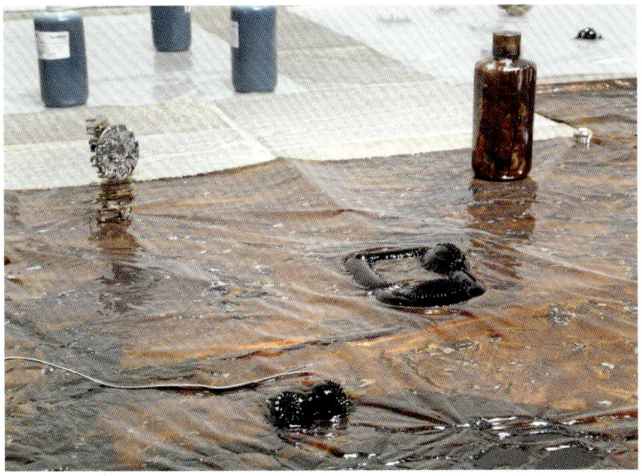
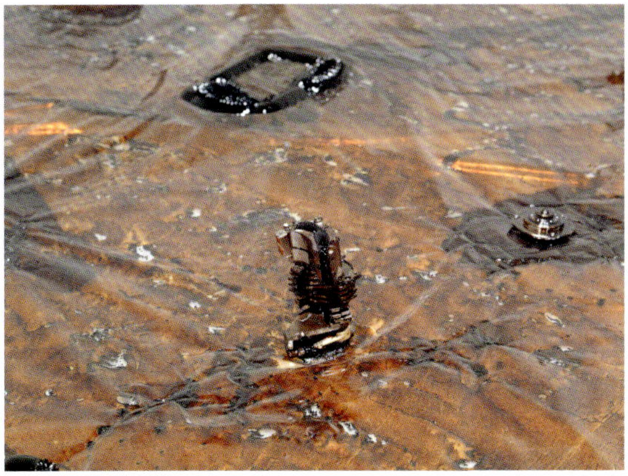
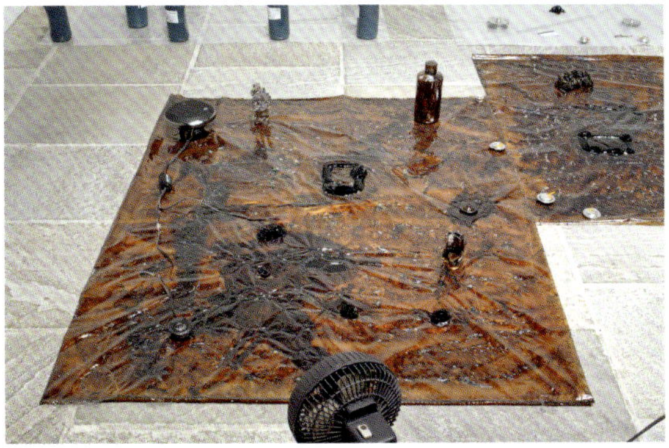
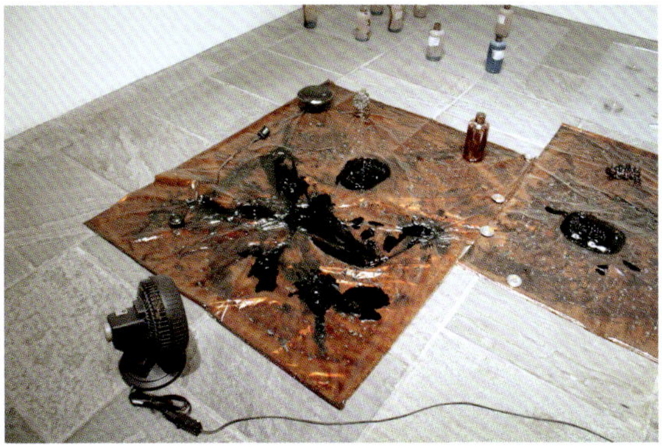

Dynamic organizations [illegible] marketplace agility th[illegible] workforce scalability [illegible]

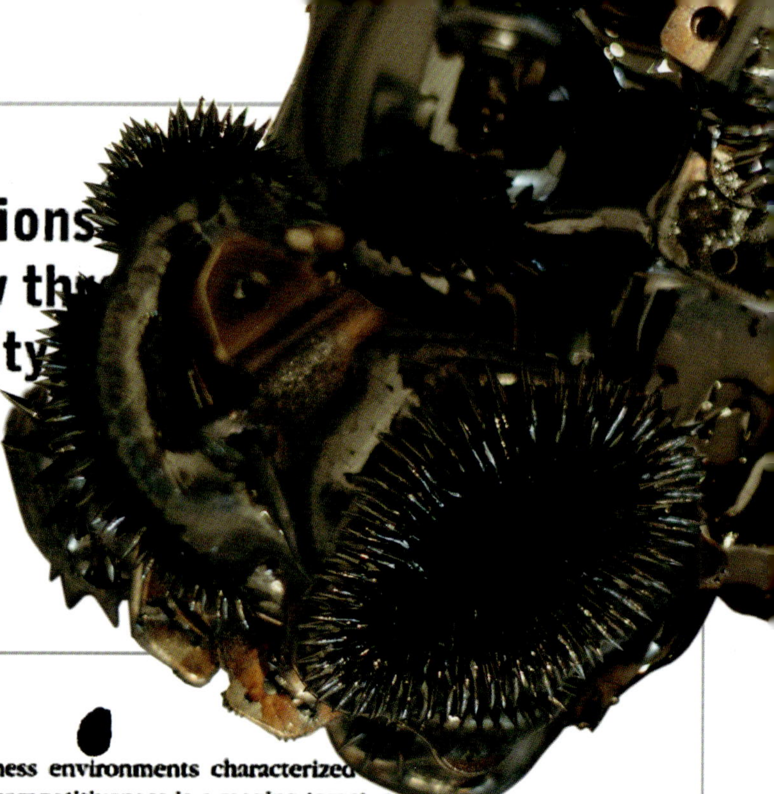

Dynamic organizations (DOs) operate in business environments characterized [illegible] frequent and discontinuous change. For them, competitiveness is a moving target, a constant pursuit of proactivity and adaptability in the marketplace, preferably undertaken as a matter of course rather than with great travail. Imagine, as Hamel and Valikangas (2003) posit, a ratio in which the numerator is the number and salience of an organization's strategic manoeuvres and the denominator reflects the time, disruption and expense required to affect those manoeuvres. A DO's challenge is to enhance the numerator by constantly attacking the marketplace with a steady stream of customized client solutions, innovative products or services or creative ways of capitalizing on existing offerings (Brown and Eisenhardt 1997; D'Aveni 1994; Ilinitch et al. 1996; Roberts 1999), even as it concurrently drives down the denominator. As Hamel and Valikangas (2003: 54) put it:

> The goal is a strategy that is forever morphing, [illegible] conforming itself to emerging opportunities and incipient trends. The goal is an organization that is constantly making its future rather than defending its past. The goal is a company where revolutionary change happens in lightning-quick, evolutionary steps – with no calamitous surprises, no convulsive reor[illegible]ations, no colossal write-offs, and no indiscriminate, across-the-board layoffs. In a tru[illegible]namic] organization, the[illegible] plenty of excitement, [illegible] no trauma.

Given these goals, it is not at all surprising that DOs tend to eschew traditional organizational forms and practices as excessively cumbersome and ossified and, alternatively, actively experiment with more nimble and flexible options ([illegible]ailbraith et al. 2002). This turn of events has opened up exciting new avenues of investigation for students of business strategy, organizational theory, leadership and the like (Peterson and Mannix 2003). So far, though, the field of strategic human resource management (SHRM) is lagging behind. Generally, the DO literature ignores or deals only superficially with people-related issues, while the SHRM literature has been slow to close the gap (Dyer and Shafer, 1999, [illegible] 2001; Wright and Snell 1998). This chapter represents a step tow[illegible] filling the void. [illegible] delineates a process whereby a

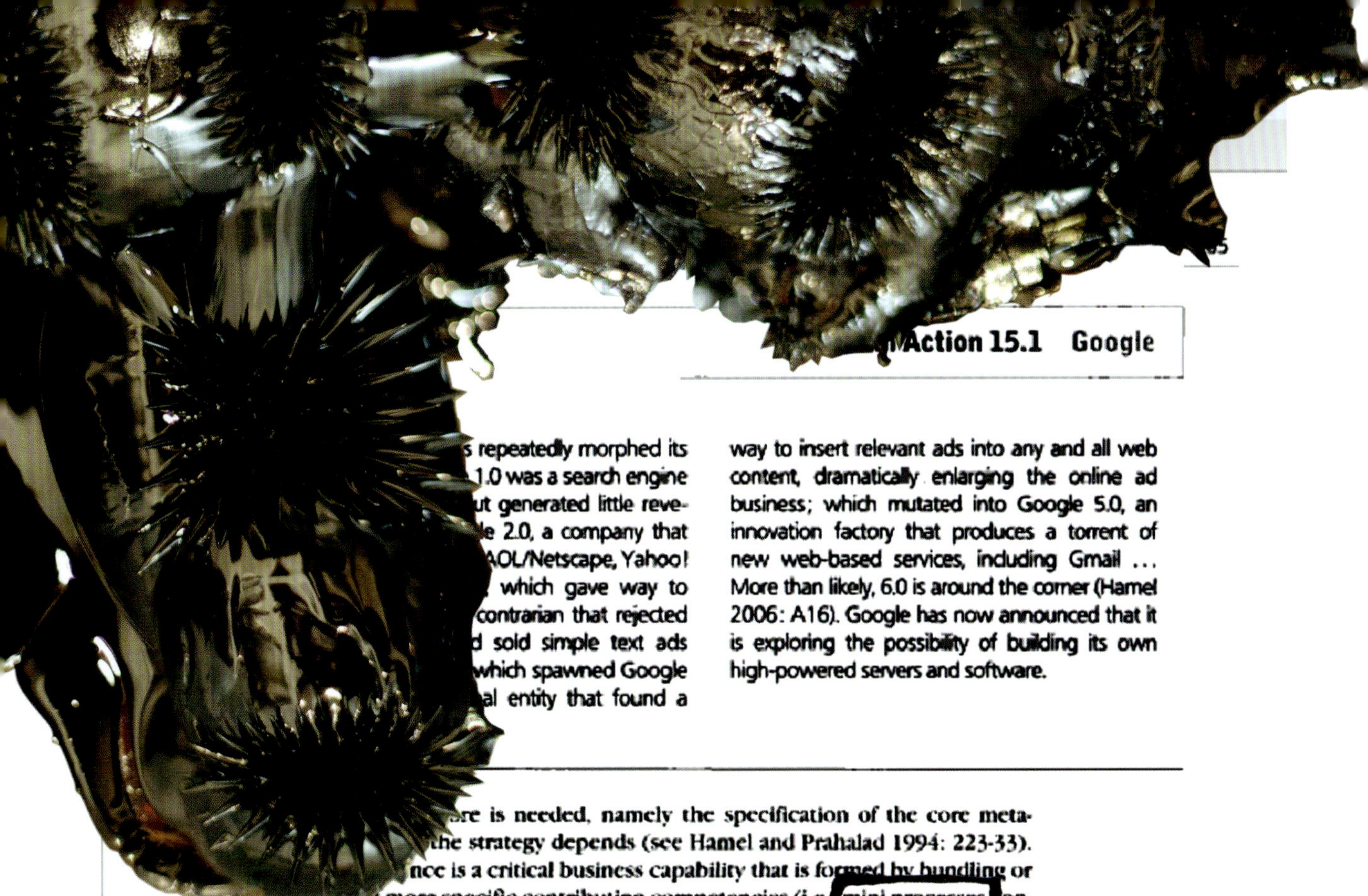

Action 15.1 Google

s repeatedly morphed its
1.0 was a search engine
ut generated little reve-
le 2.0, a company that
AOL/Netscape, Yahoo!
, which gave way to
contrarian that rejected
d sold simple text ads
which spawned Google
al entity that found a

way to insert relevant ads into any and all web content, dramatically enlarging the online ad business; which mutated into Google 5.0, an innovation factory that produces a torrent of new web-based services, including Gmail ... More than likely, 6.0 is around the corner (Hamel 2006: A16). Google has now announced that it is exploring the possibility of building its own high-powered servers and software.

re is needed, namely the specification of the core meta- the strategy depends (see Hamel and Prahalad 1994: 223-33). nce is a critical business capability that is fo[redacted] or [redacted] of more speci[redacted] competencies (i.e. mini-processes consisting of particular skills and technologies). Logistics, for example is a core meta-competence for Federal Express, while scheduling and package tracking are two essential contributing co[redacted]

Essentially, a DO is an ever-changing portfolio of ventures. In pursuit of marketplace agility, the requisite core meta-competence, then, is the capacity to effectively and efficiently steer these [redacted] of four contributing competencies: exploration, exploitation, adaptation and exit. Exploration involves the generation and testing of new ideas. Exploitation is how some of these ideas are transformed into solutions, products or services to be quickly delivered to the marketplace before competitors catch on and catch up. It is the point at which a D[redacted] competitive advantages to generate revenues. The exploration-exploitation dyad is alw[redacted]nage (March 1991; M[redacted] is made even more so in dynamic situations by the barrage of disruptive forces emanating from [redacted] and other sources. Thus the need fo[redacted] contributing competency: adaptation – the process of spotting emerging threats early and mounting immediate [redacted] necessary (Haeckel 1999; Lewin and Volberda 1999). Even a DO that is superb at adapting, however, knows that nothing is forever, so it must be not only willing, [redacted] to abandon unpromising ideas and even to cannibalize its own marketplace offerings on a timely basis without hesitancy or remorse (Foster and Kaplan 2001; Horn et al. 2006). This is the fourth contributing competency: exit.

Figure 15.1 shows a fictional DO that at Time 1 consisted of eight ventures spread around the renewal cycle. By time 2, this number had dropped to seven [redacted], four survivors [redacted] 1 – all of which had transitioned to different places on the cycle – and three new ones. Snapshots taken at Times 3, 4, and so on would, of course, reveal [redacted] different patterns [redacted]s this firm demonstrating the requisite core meta-competen[redacted]' if the portfolios of ventures that

Workforce scalability

Workforce scalability is the term we use to capture the capacity of an organization to keep its human resources aligned on an ongoing basis by constantly transitioning from one human resource configuration to another and another, ad infinitum, on a timely basis and in a seamless way (Dyer and Ericksen 2005). At this point, we expand on this definition [illegible] basic concepts from the resource-based view (Barney 1991), show how the construct helps to deliver a sustained competitive advantage [illegible]
dynamic situations.

Workforce scalability defined

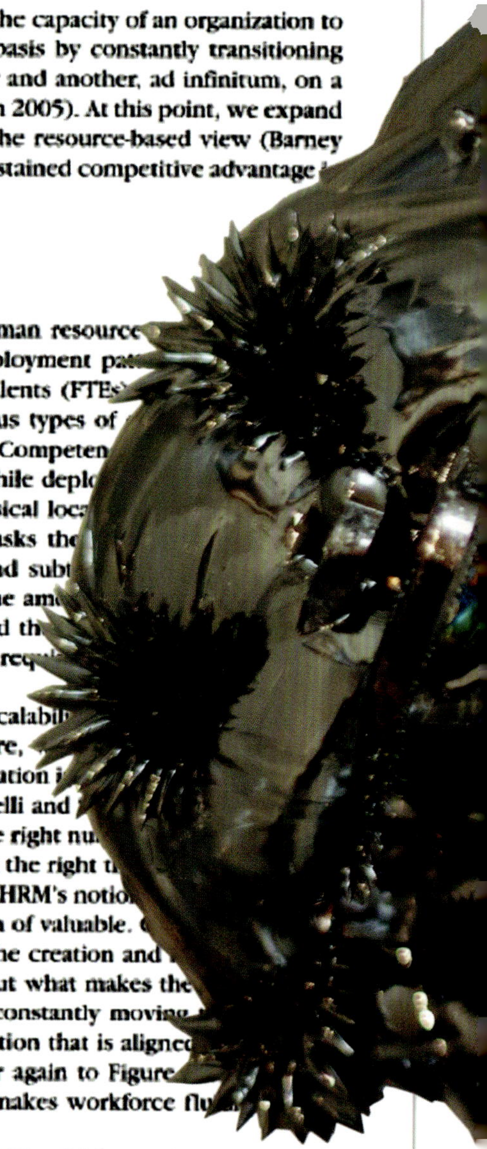

Workforce scalability indicates the evolution of human resource
four dimensions: headcount, competence mix, deployment pa
contributions. Headcount refers to full-time equivalents (FTEs
number of employees (including regular and various types of
times the number of hours these people work. Competen
employees' knowledge and skills are distributed, while deplo
their assignments across organizational and/or physical loca
butions relate to the organizational value of the tasks the
again to Figure 15.1. As this fictitious firm adds and subt
teams and team memberships over time, imagine the am
in FTEs, competence requirements, assignments and th
add value. Successfully meeting these ever-changing req
scalability is all about.

As [illegible] suggests, workforce scalabil
nents: alignment and fluidity. [illegible] the SHRM literature,
exists [illegible]n resource configuration i
uration required by its business strategy (e.g. Cappelli and
Jackson 1987) or, put differently, when a firm has the right nu
of people in the right places at the right times doing the right t
Ericksen 2005; Dyer and Holder 1988). Notice that SHRM's notio
right correspond to the resource-based view's notion of valuable.
all refer to a workforce's capacity to contribute to the creation and
of successful strategic thrusts in the marketplace. But what makes the
special is that for a DO, workforce alignment is a constantly movin
ever-changing circumstances, a workforce configuration that is aligned
in time is unlikely to remain so for very long (refer again to Figure
course, ups the ante on workforce alignment and makes workforce flu
more crucial.

Workforce fluidity refers to the speed and ease with which transitions are made from one aligned human resource [illegible] another and then another and another, ad infinitum. As suggested earlier, workforce fluidity helps a DO achieve workforce alignment (Wright and Snell 1998), even as [illegible] the denominator in Hamel and Valikangas's (2003) ratio by minimizing the friction and pain otherwise associated with constant adjustments [illegible] mixes, deployment patterns and employee contributions.

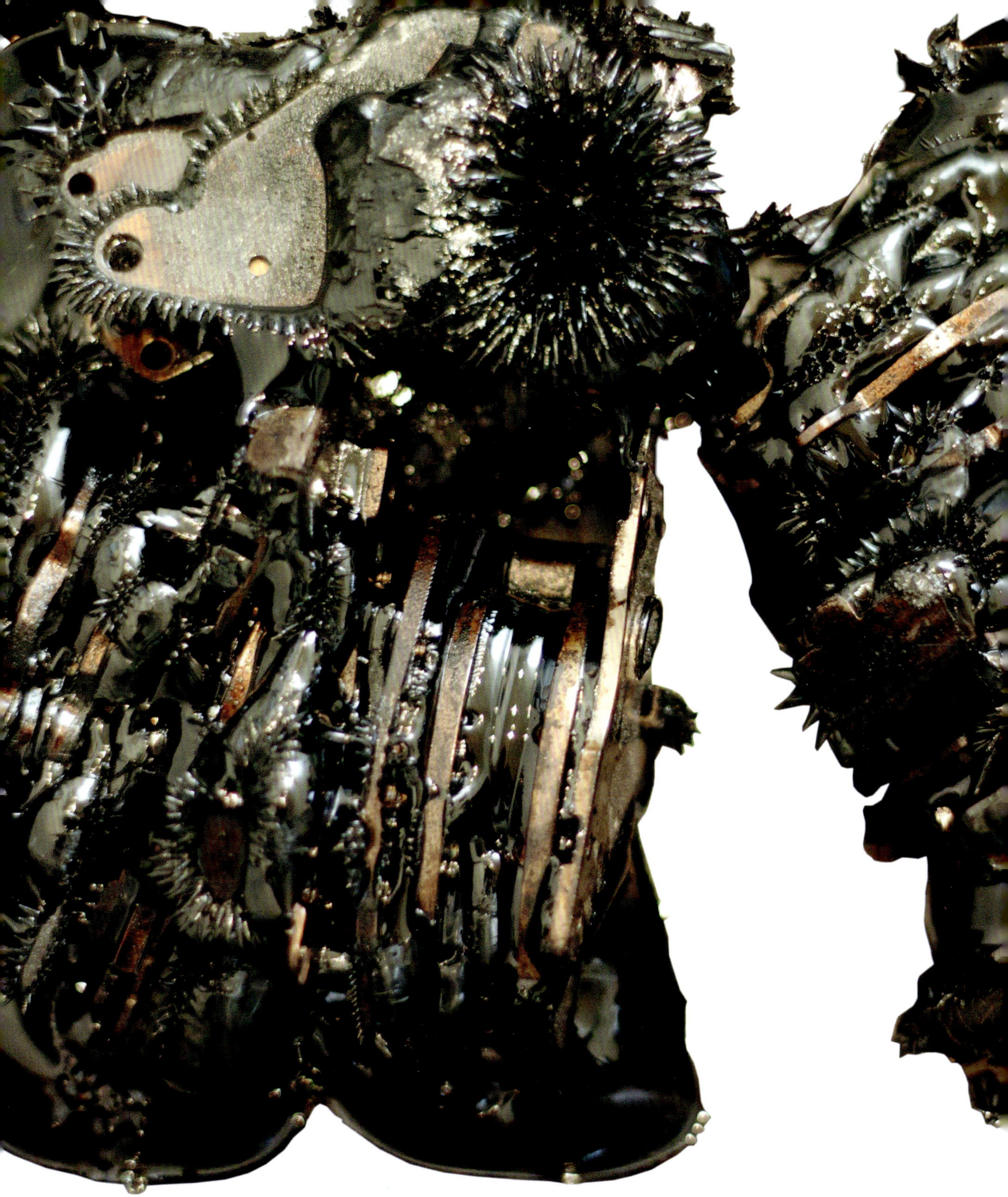

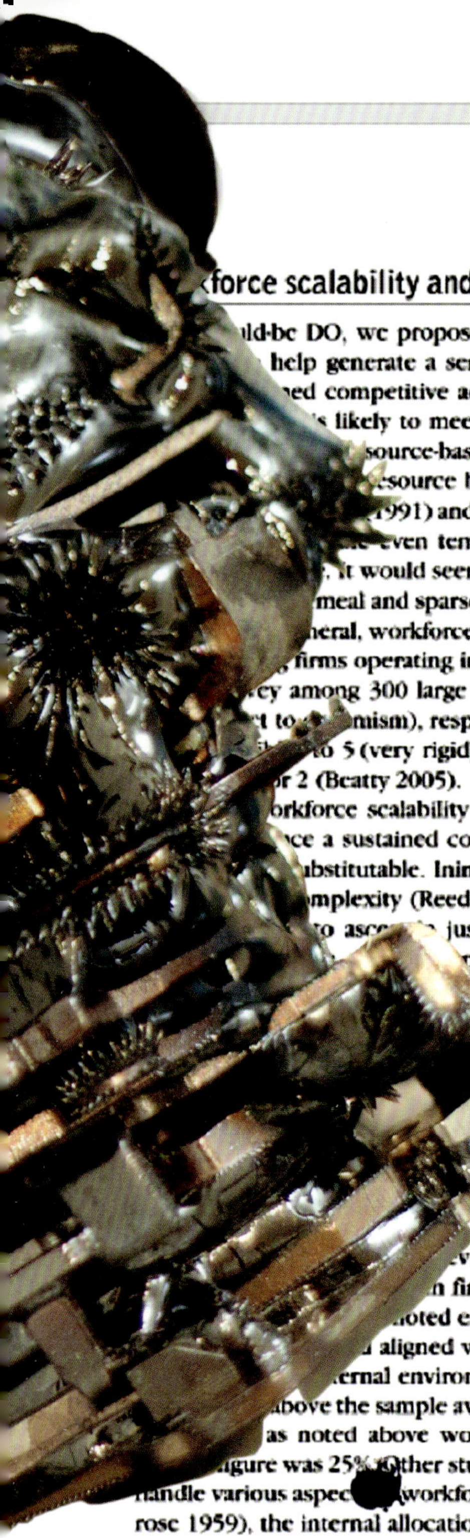

‹force scalability and sustained competitive advantage

ıld-be DO, we propose, workforce scalability is a resource with the clear help generate a series of temporary competitive advantages and, over ned competitive advantage. This is because, for any given firm, work- s likely to meet all four of the necessary and sufficient conditions source-based view of the firm (Barney 2001). The baseline esource be valuable, which by definition (and thus tautologi- 991) and Priem and Butler (2001) debate), workforce scalabil- even temporary competitive advantages a valuable resource , it would seem that workforce scalability is, although the available meal and sparse. In a study of 196 small businesses, Ericksen (2006) neral, workforce alignment was relatively rare, but that it was particu- firms operating in comparatively dynamic environments. Further, in a ey among 300 large US and European companies (alas, undifferentiated t to mism), respondents rated the fluidity of their firms on a scale of to 5 (very rigid). The mean response was 3.38 and only 15% rated r 2 (Beatty 2005).

orkforce scalability is a valuable and rare resource, this is insufficient ce a sustained competitive advantage. For this, it also must be inimi- ıbstitutable. Inimitability stems from a confluence of causal ambigu- mplexity (Reed and DeFillippi 1990). The former makes it difficult to asc just how a DO achieved workplace scalability, while penden makes it unlikely that an approach that y in others. Logic, as well as the aforemen- ests that workplace scalability is indeed diffi- e know of no evidence directly relating to this IBM, are attempting to use technology to obvi- of workforce scalability, especially geographic her than doing things the other way around hich this might negate the capacity of work- ned competitive advantage, however, remains to

vidence to suggest that the components of workforce n firm performance, especially in dynamic situations. In oted earlier, Ericksen (2006) focused part of his analysis on aligned workforces and found that among those operating in ernal environments the average annual increase in revenues was bove the sample average. Among those operating in volatile circumstan- as noted above workforce alignment was rarer), the comparable sale igure was 25%. Other studies have documented how ineffectively many firms handle various aspec workforce fluidity – e.g. the accession of new recruits (Penrose 1959), the internal allocation of employees (Henderson and Clark 1990; Tripsas 1997), and the release of non-performing and redundant employees (Cascio 2002) – and the resulting deleterious effects on organizational adaptation and change. recent case study, summarized in Table 15.1, illustrates how Yahoo's ability to achieve elements of workforce scalability contributed to its attainment of competitive advantage over Excite in the early years of the fast paced world of web-based search (Rindova and Kotha 2001).

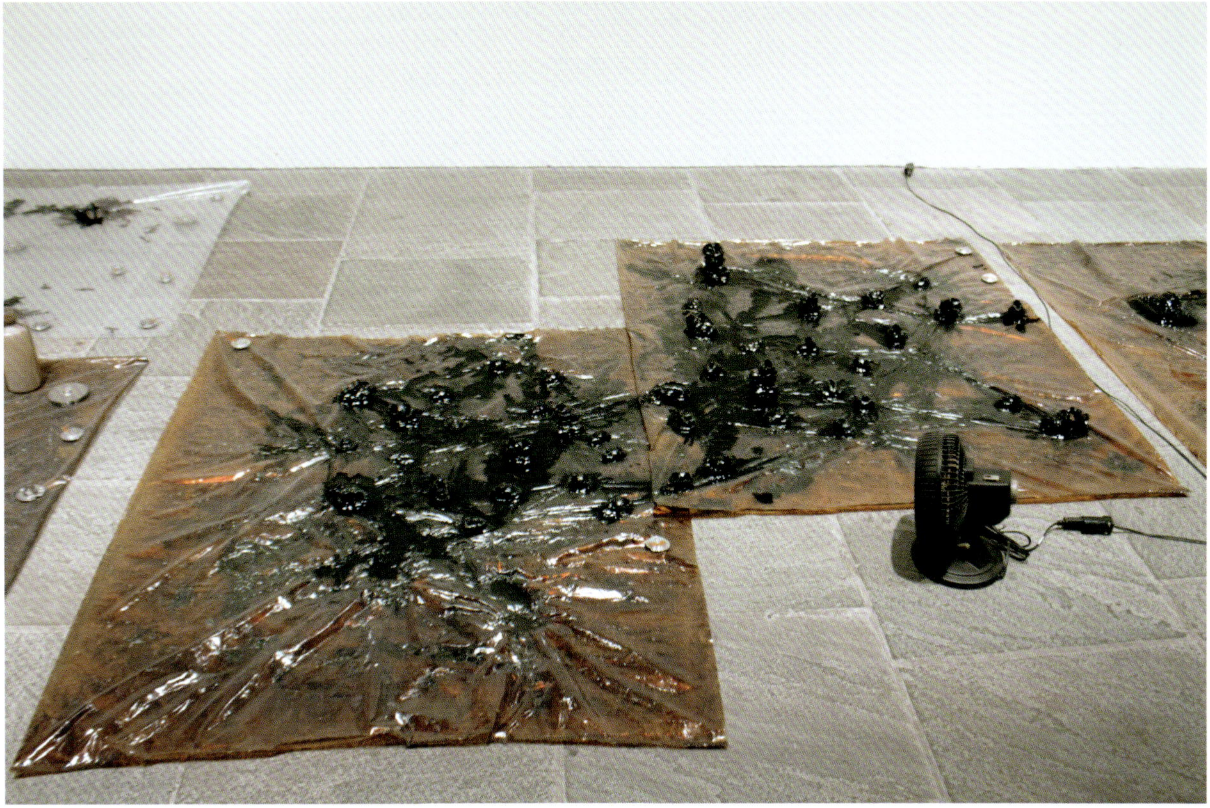

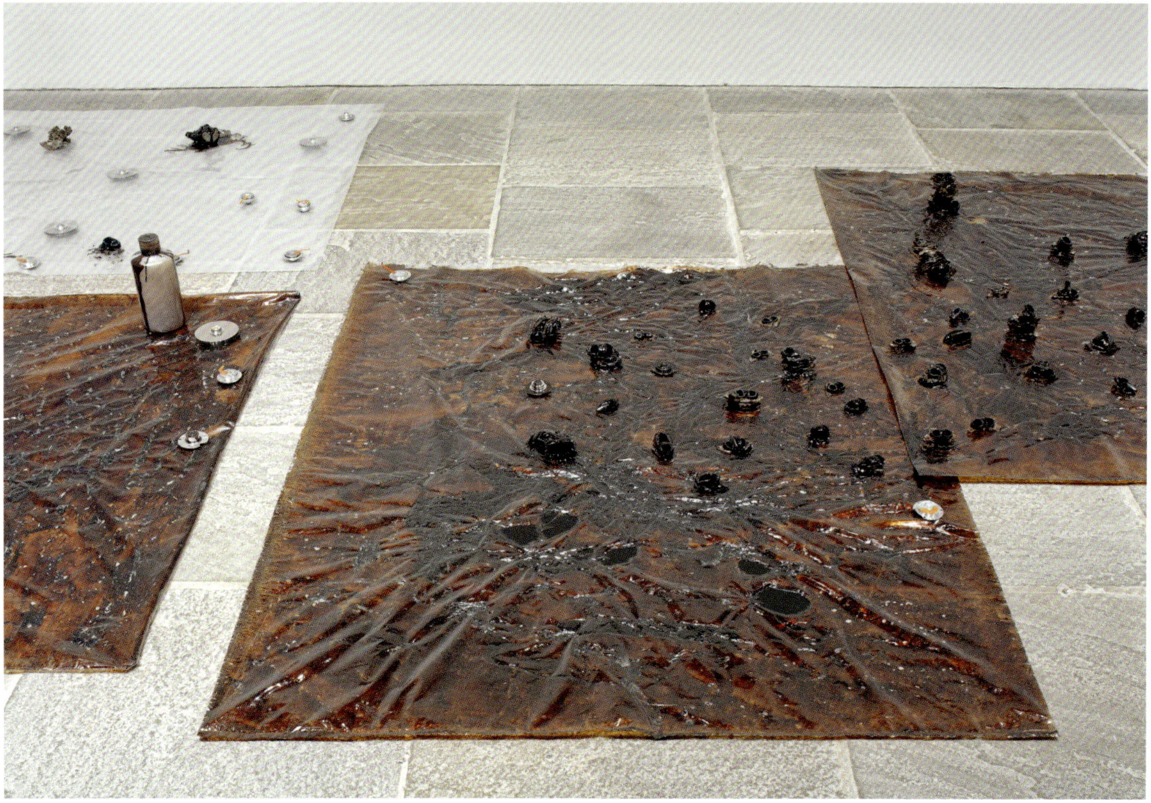

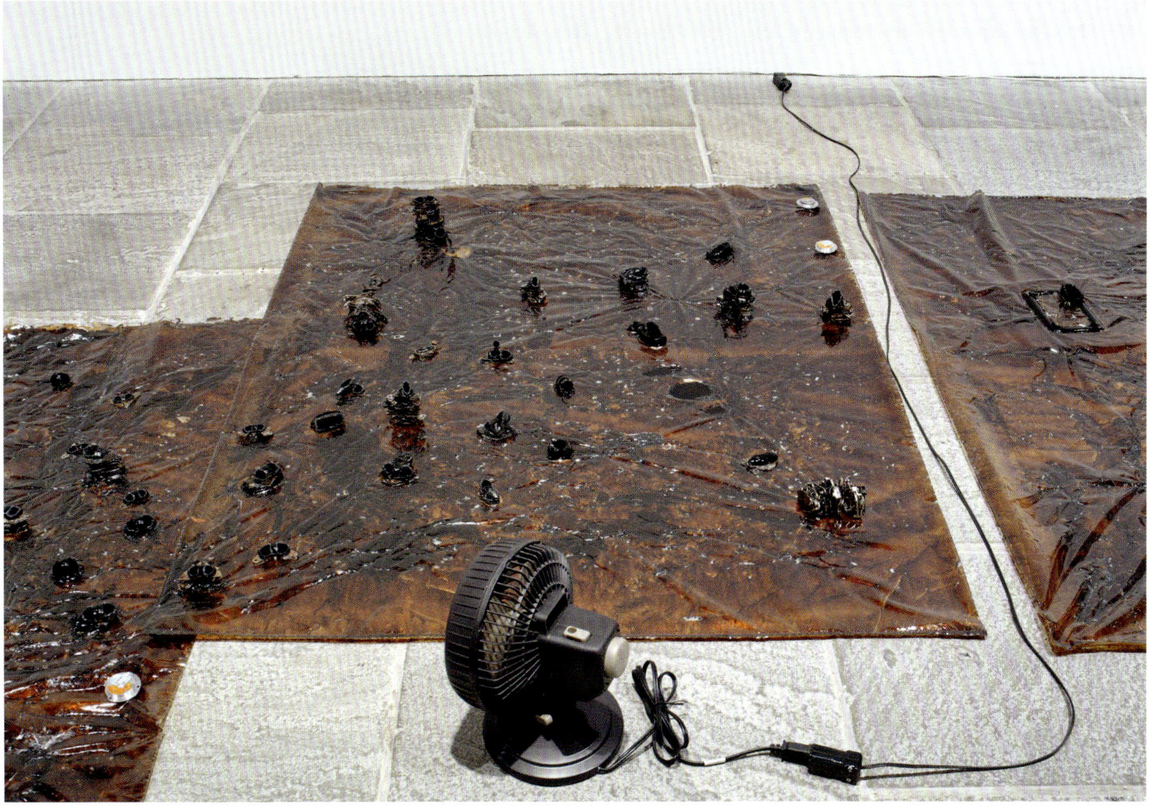

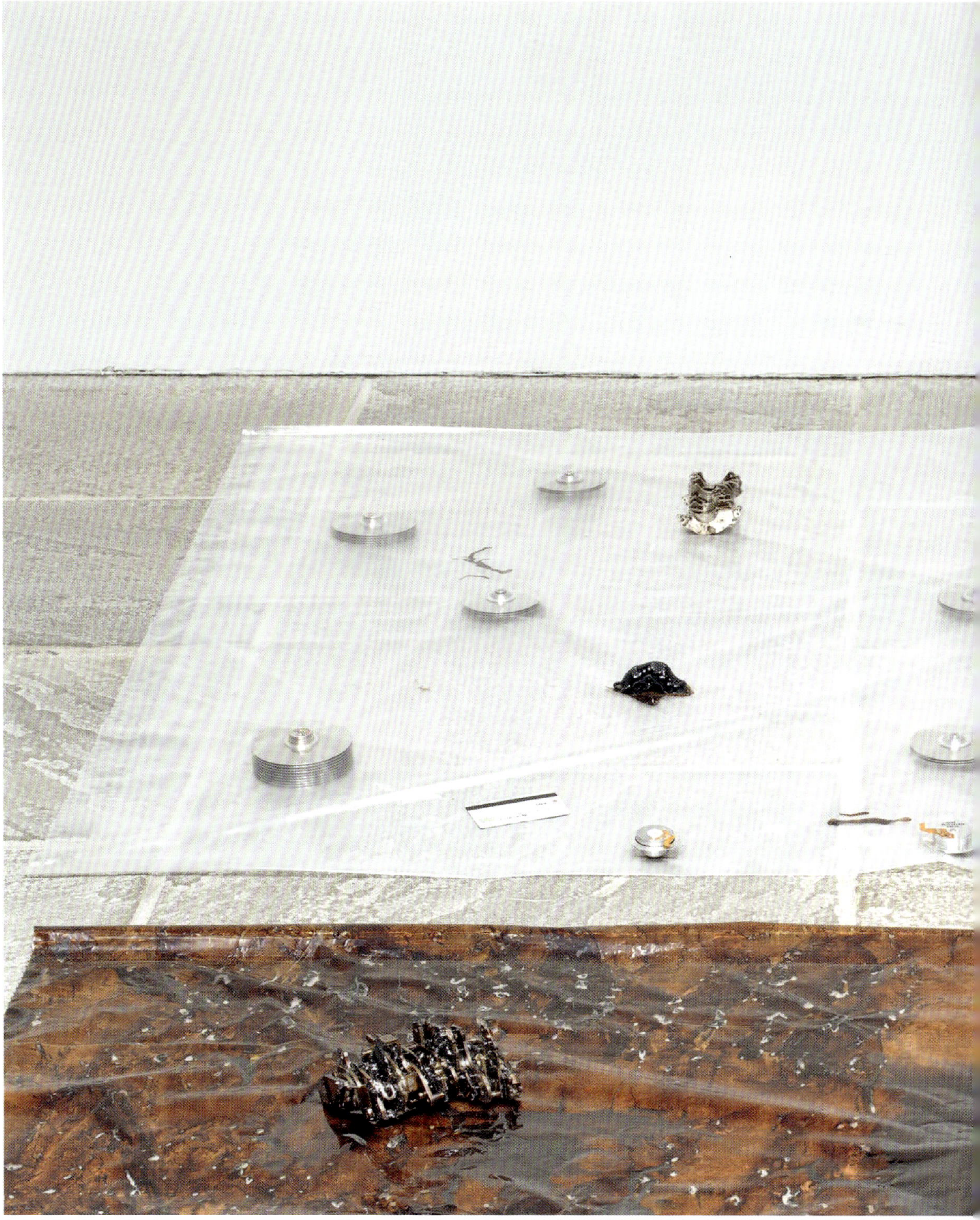

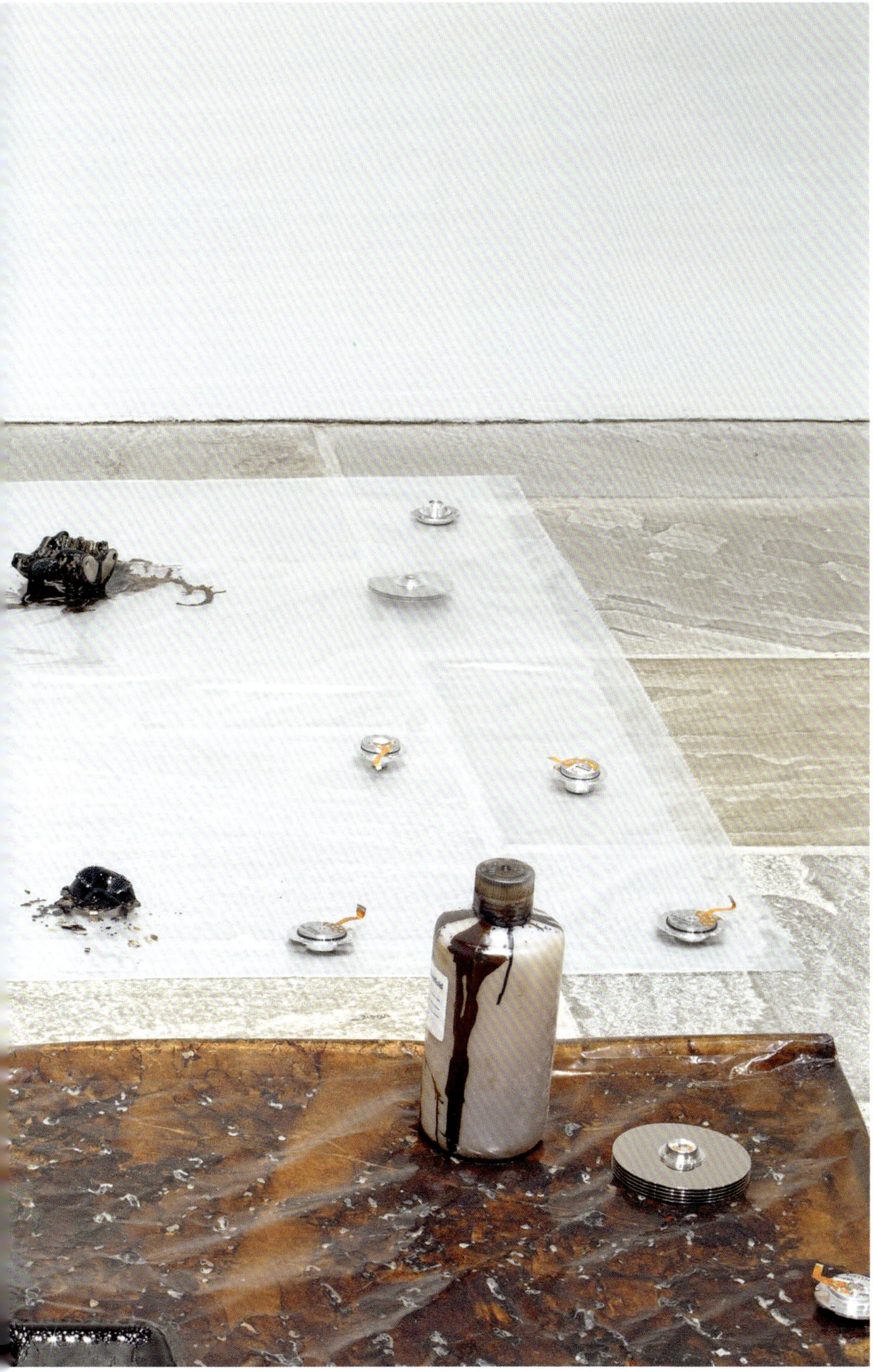

Figure 15.1 **A DOs meta-competence**

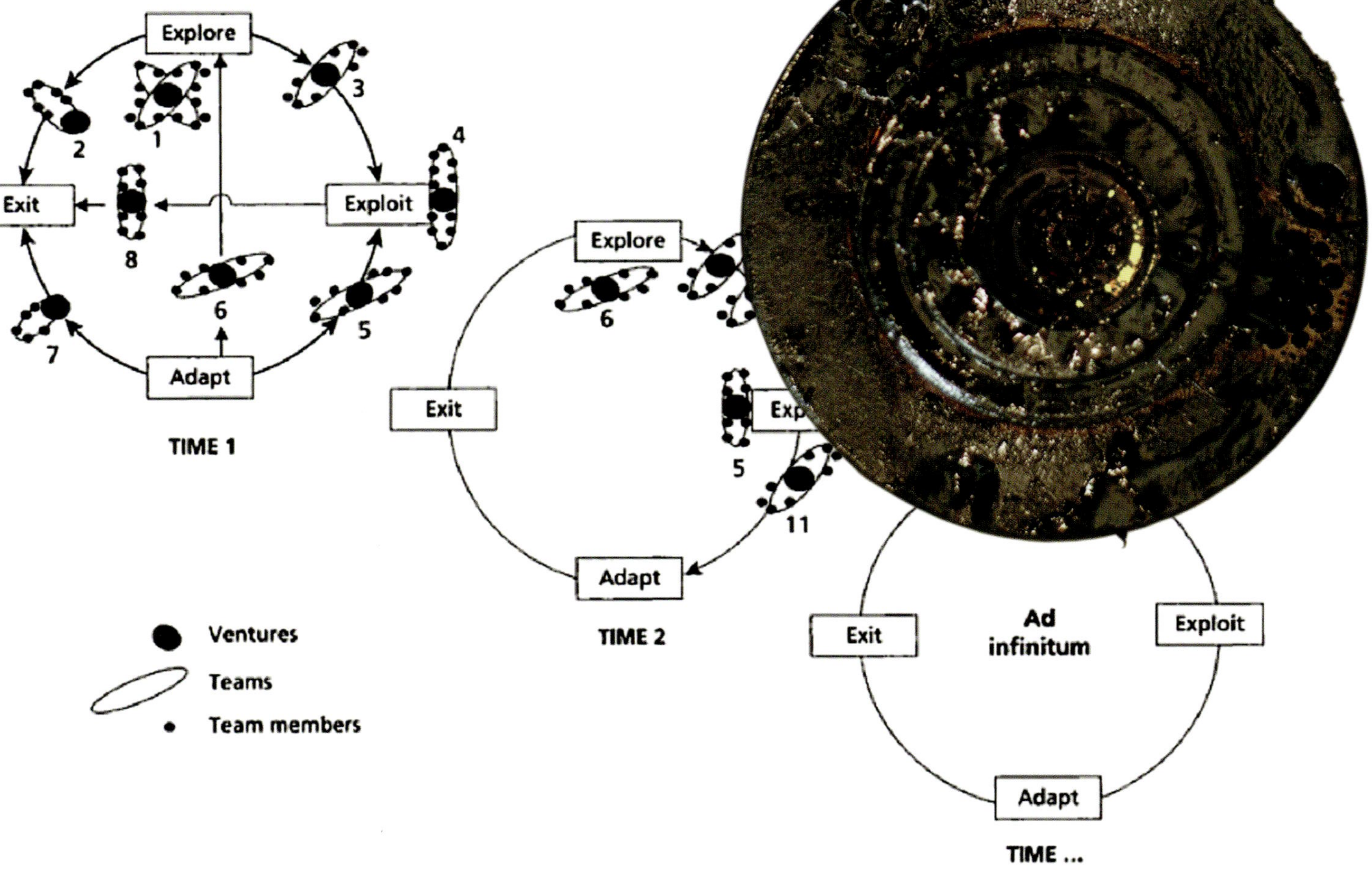

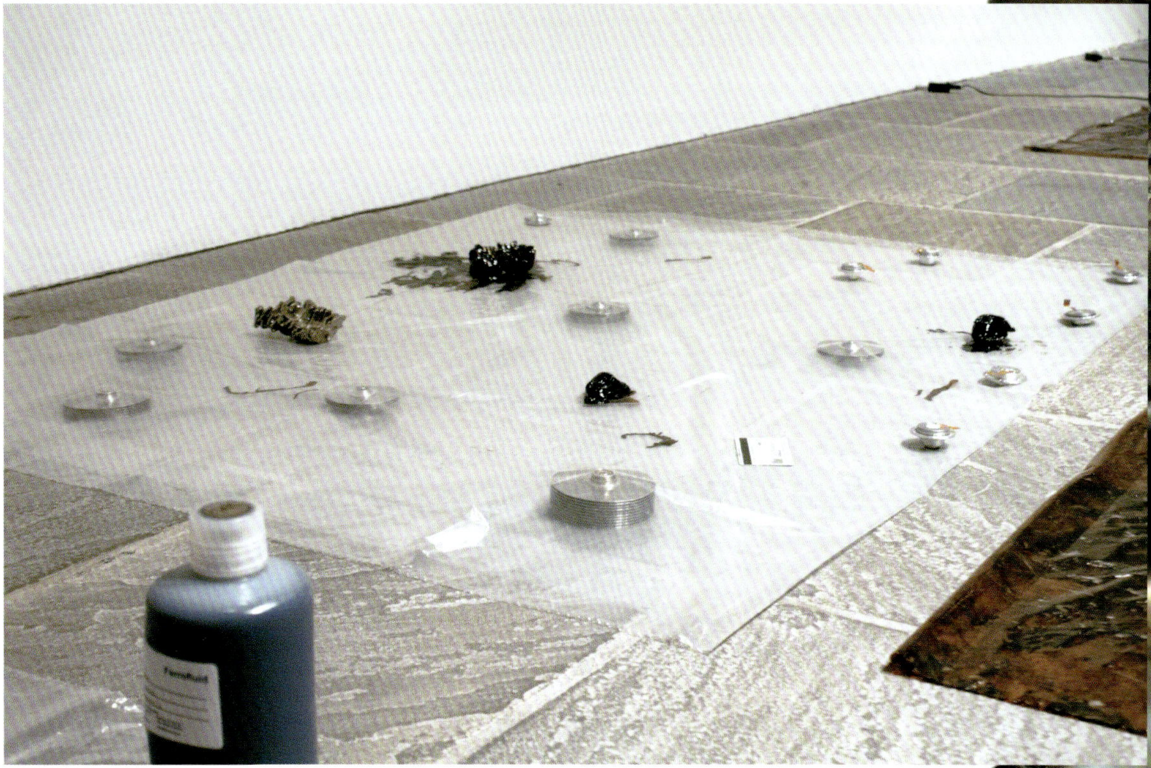
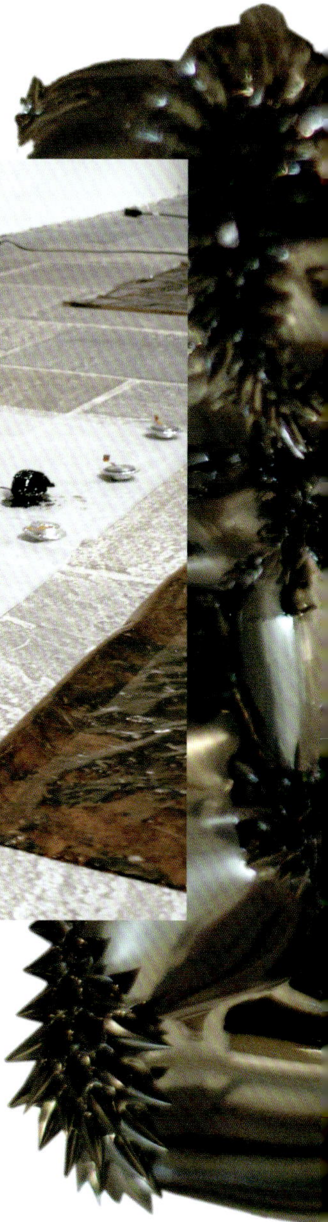

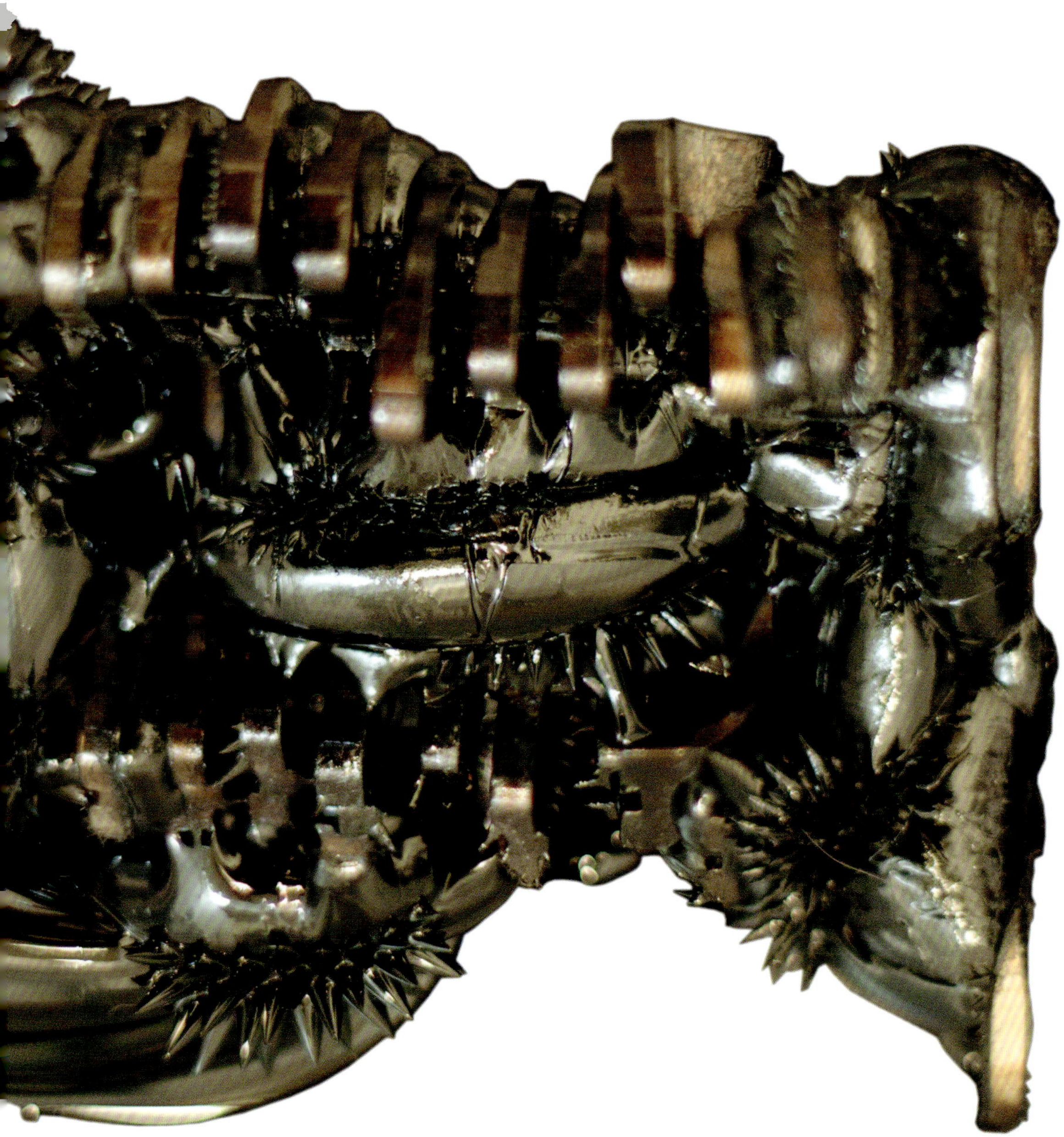

Table 15.1 Workforce scalability as a source of sustained competitive advantage

[redacted]

	[redacted]	[redacted]	[redacted]
[redacted]	[redacted]	[redacted] Content [redacted]	[redacted]
[redacted]	[redacted] 'surfers' [redacted]	[redacted] surfers, [redacted] 'Surfers' [redacted] content [redacted] content [redacted]	[redacted]
[redacted]	[redacted] skilled pool [redacted]	[redacted] 'surfers' [redacted]	[redacted]
[redacted]	[redacted]		

What remains to be done, however, is research that focuses on the full scope of workforce scalability. There is a need for studies that include both workforce alignment and workforce fluidity (all four d [redacted] between them, but also the issue [redacted] value, rarity, inimitability and non-substitutability directly. Then there is the 'so wha [redacted] levels of workforce scalability also realize temporary and/or sustained competitive advantages in the marketplace and achieve superior financial results?

Our analysis and the limited data available suggest that for any given DO, attaining ... ely to be a work in progress for ... now for sure how to do it and

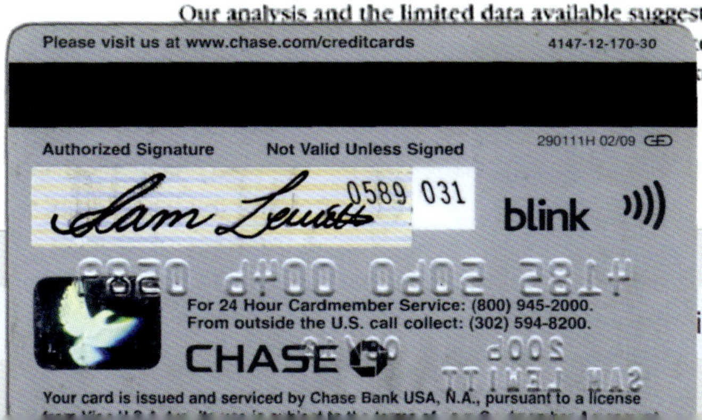

iew.

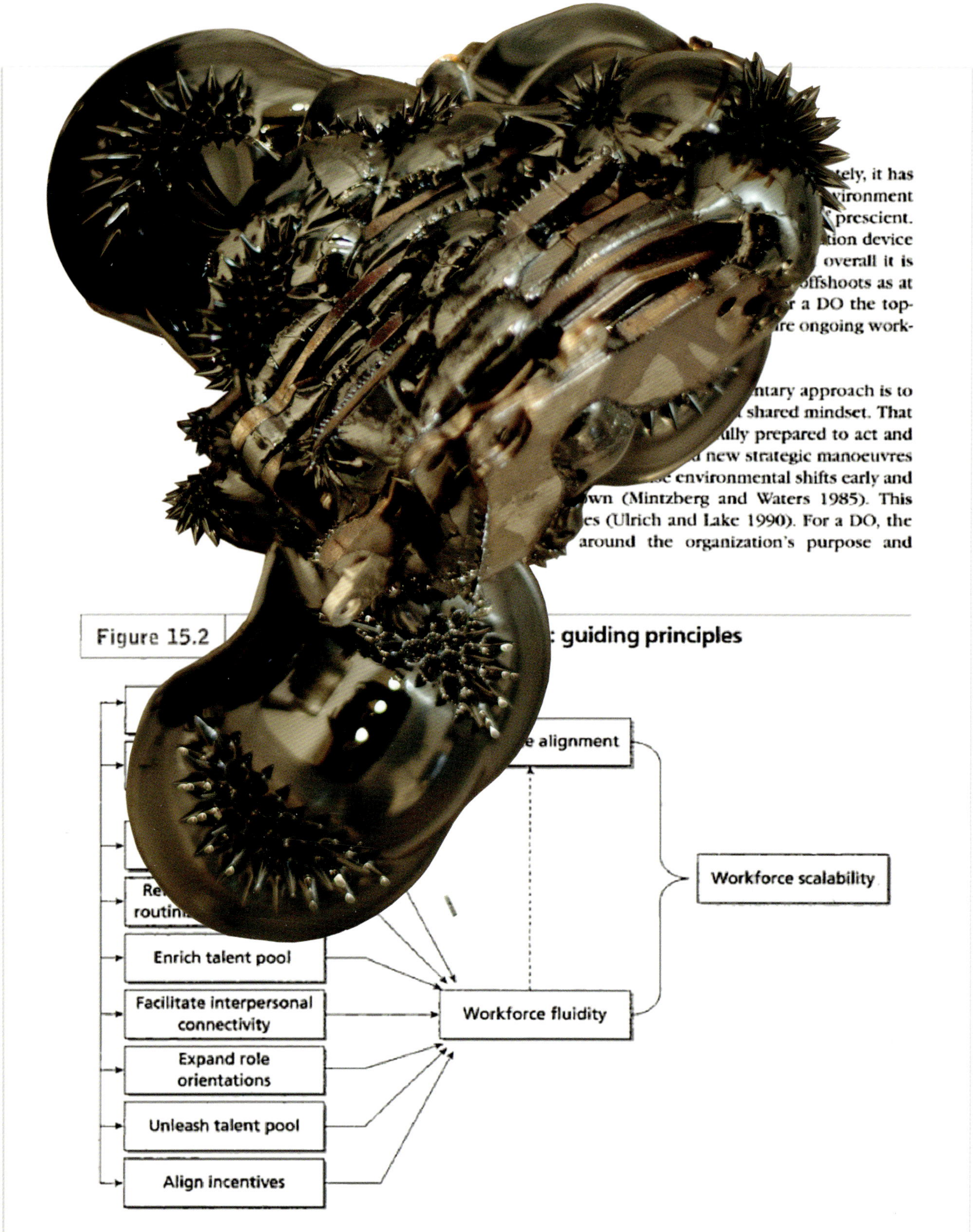
tely, it has
vironment
prescient.
tion device
overall it is
offshoots as at
a DO the top-
re ongoing work-
ntary approach is to
shared mindset. That
ully prepared to act and
new strategic manoeuvres
environmental shifts early and
wn (Mintzberg and Waters 1985). This
es (Ulrich and Lake 1990). For a DO, the
around the organization's purpose and
Figure 15.2
guiding principles
alignment
Workforce scalability
routin
Enrich talent pool
Facilitate interpersonal connectivity
Workforce fluidity
Expand role orientations
Unleash talent pool
Align incentives

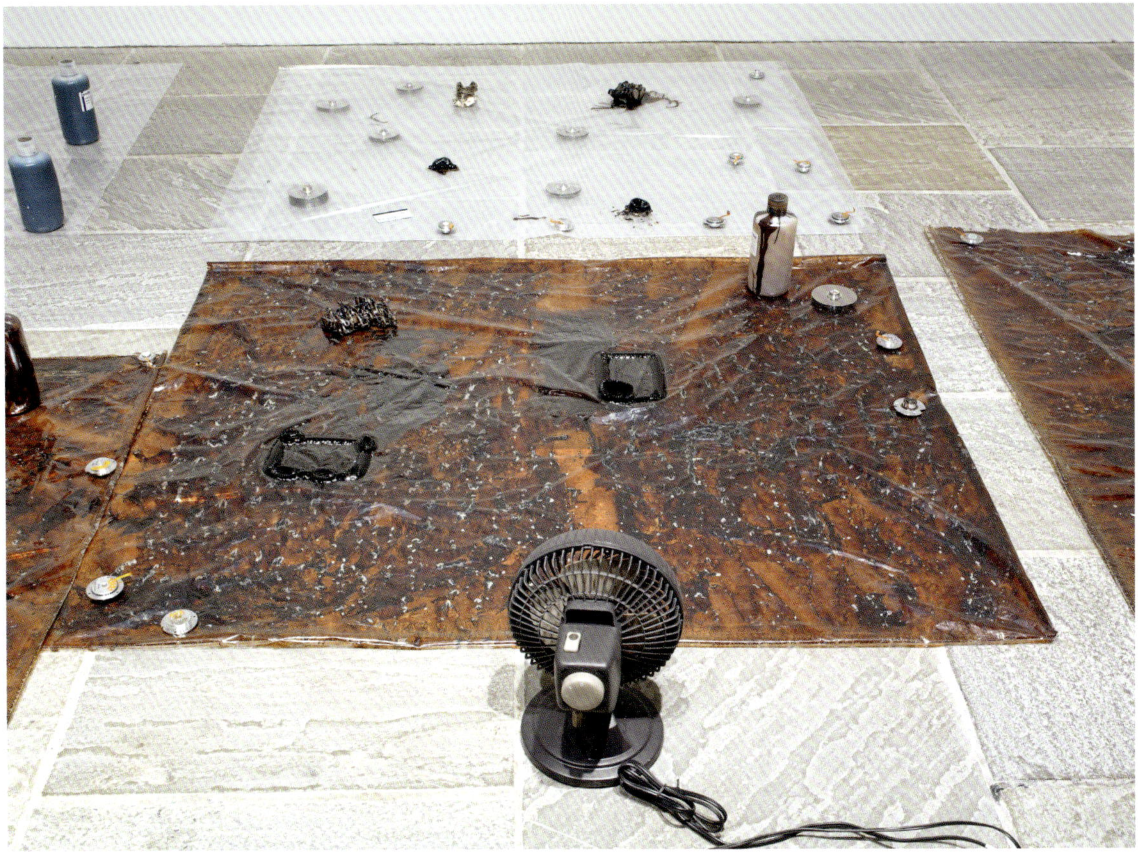

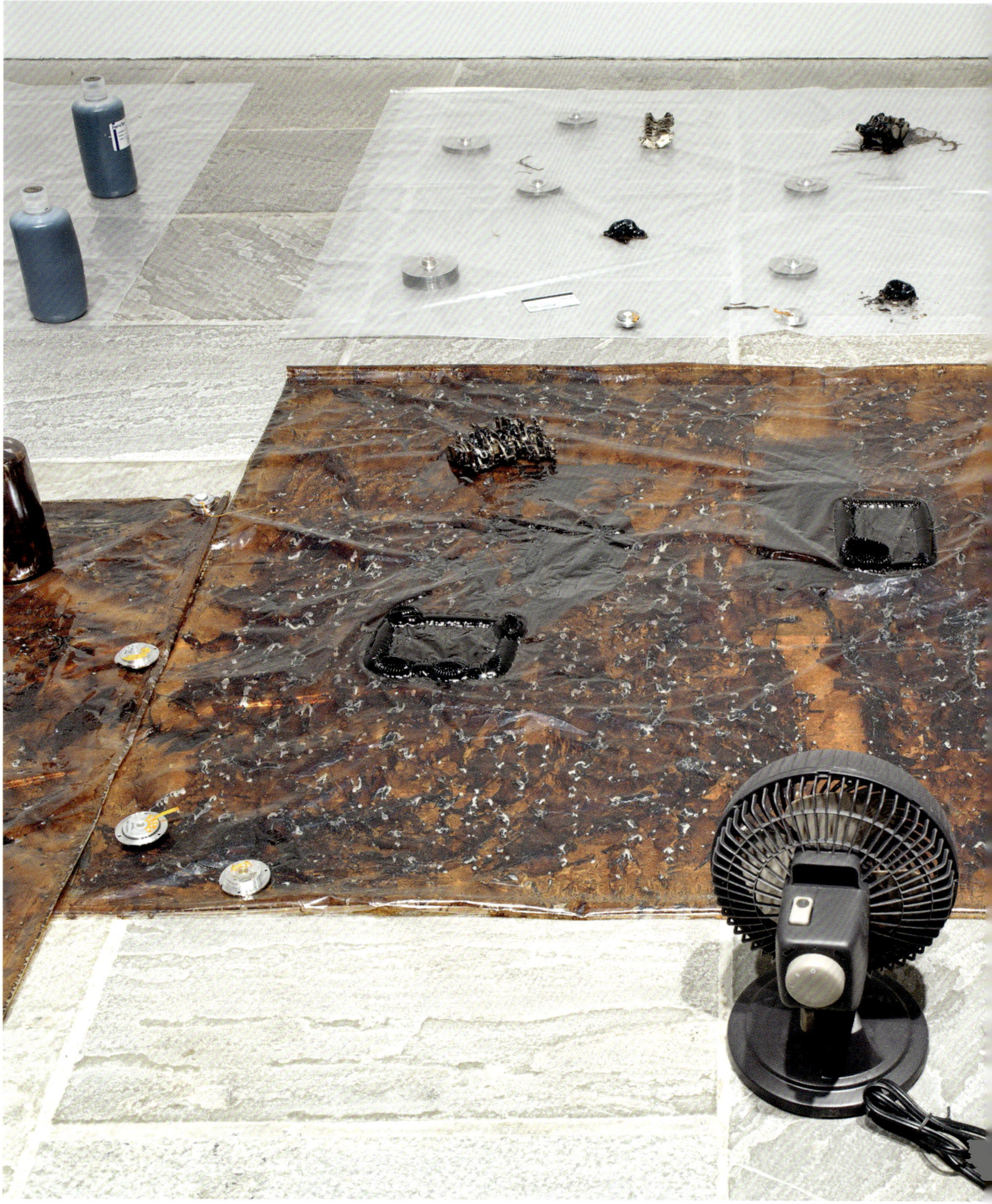

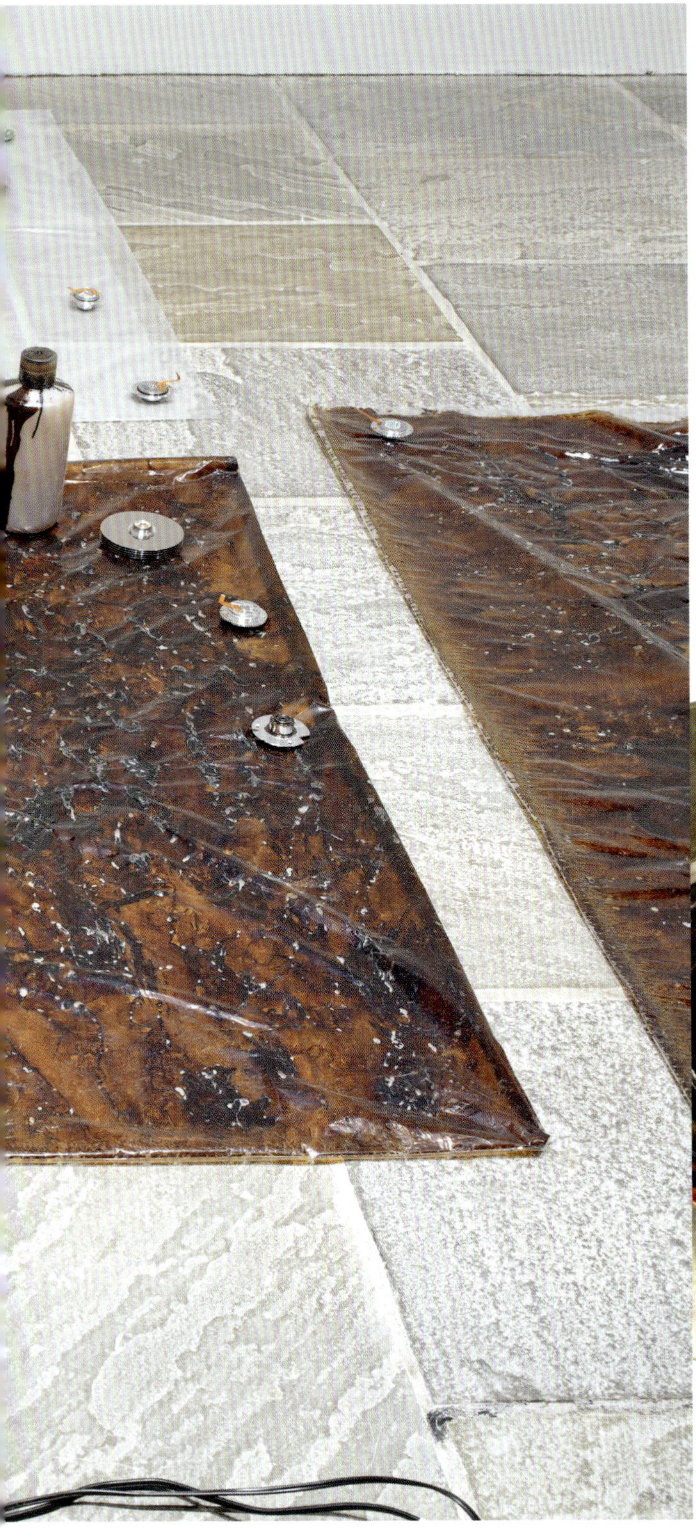
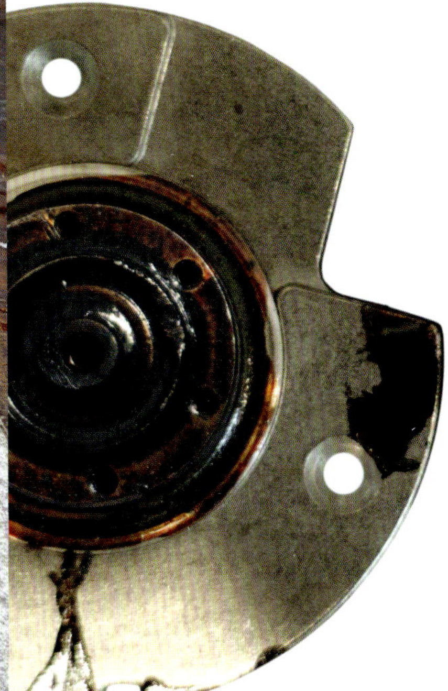

processes in a way that actively encourages and facilitates ongoing workforce alignment. The two key sub-principles are:

- create a common cause
- embed contextual clarity.

The creation of a common cause requires the articulation of [redacted] organizational vision [redacted]r mission that is both aspirational and inspirational – as Google has done with its well-known mantra 'To organize the world's knowledge' – and then clearly communicating it over and over in many different ways. The idea is to keep employees focused and fired up by making it perfectly clear what the firm exists to do and why this is a good thing for it, them and society. But employees also need to know where they fit in, which is why it is also essential to embed contextual clarity. This process begins with the articulation of the firm's business model(s) in a way that paints a complete picture of its environment, how it operates, what it takes for it to succeed and the crucial role that employees play in the grand scheme of things. It continues with efforts to assure that the business model is clearly understood and consensually internalized by all employees (potential techniques include surround communication, open-book management and commitment management – see Dyer and Shafer 2003; Galbraith et al. 2002).

Driven by a common cause and informed with contextual clarity, a DO's [redacted]ell positioned to [redacted]nd the reasons behi[redacted] sudden changes [redacted] business plans an[redacted]o adapt accordingly [redacted]qually important, they [redacted]withal required to [redacted] environmental changes on their own, to use this information to make timely and appropriate adjustments in business plans or to instigate new ones and to do whatever they need to do to assure they are realigned with the new business situation.

Pursuing workforce fluidity

[redacted]orkforce fluidity is to assure that all employee moves [redacted]behavioural adjustments [redacted]hether they involve a single individual o[redacted]group of e[redacted]ssly and efficiently. A step in the ri[redacted]ecti[redacted]s, is to do a good job of operationalizing the foregoing princip[redacted]s. Flexible planning [redacted]nd a shared minds[redacted]t grease the skids [redacted]f workforce transitions. B[redacted] this. Additiona[redacted]to the facilitation of external staffing (i.e., the addition and removal of people) and internal transitions.

Evidence suggests that firms often stumble when trying to use external staffing and internal transitions simultaneously (Anderson 2001; Brockner 1992; Charness and Levine 2002; Penrose 1959). In the small business study cited earlier this was indeed the case for firms operat[redacted] stable environments, [redacted]ut not for those operating in comparativ[redacted]y dynamic environments [redacted]. Among the latter, holding the effects of [redacted]nt at high levels, firms that used both approaches concurrently increased their revenues by 34% annually, whereas those that shied away from this two-pronged approach had average annual revenue growth of about 20%. While hardly definitive, these data nonetheless suggest that for a DO the capacity to simultaneously employ external staffing and internal

I[illegible] a well-oiled outplacement process[illegible] probably in partnership with an external firm, th[illegible] extensive job search assistance and a generous severance package and does so in a way that employees perceive as fair and just. Studies suggest that the treatment received by laid off and terminated employees has a significant impact on survivors' willingness to adapt to future organizational changes and on their subsequent job performance (e.g., Brockner et al. 1994; Naumann et al. 1995).

Internal transitions: guiding principles

Theory and research suggest that internal transitions – whether self- or organizationally initiated – are more likely to occur when employees individually and collectively have the capability (C) required to make the moves and adjustments, as well as the unfettered opportunity (O) and desire or motivation ([illegible] pose, C is enhanced by operationalizing two principl[illegible]nrich the talent pool[illegible]d facilitate interpersonal connectivi[illegible] ples – expand role orientations [illegible]d unleash the talent pool[illegible] and M is facilitated by operationalizing a single princip[illegible]dition to the motivation provided by the firm's mission statement and the intrinsically motivating aspects of expanded opportunities).

Enrich the talent pool. A DO needs employees who possess broad competence profiles and behavioural repertoires (Wright and Snell 1998). The [illegible]ing the talent pool begins with the selection of employees for bo[illegible] diversity and fit. Diversity here refers not only to race and gender, but also to the bac[illegible]ences, knowledge and skills that new recruits bring to the firm. The search is for employees who, individually and collectively, bring a variety of perspectives, as well as foundational aptitudes on which they can build over time (Wright and Snell 1998). At the same time, somewhat paradoxically, a DO must screen for cultural fit to find employees whose personality traits and attitudes indicate a preference for change over stability and proactivity over passivity (Unsworth and Parker 2003). Consider [illegible]'s hiring process which has been described as 'grueling . . . akin to a Mensa test [illegible]alues nonconformi[illegible] given to candidates who [illegible] weird avocatio[illegible] out-of-the-ordinary experiences' (Hamel 2006: A16). 'Goo[illegible] website (www.Google.com) says, 'range from former neurosurgeons, CEOs, and U.S. puzzle champions to alligator wrestlers and former marines . . . [who] . . . make for interesting cube mates.'

Once the right types of employee are on board, enriching the talent pool becomes a matter of fostering serial incompetence. 'In the face of change', Godin (2000) reminds us, 'the competent are helpless'. Competent employees are those who are an inch wide and a mile deep. They excel at applying sharply honed techniques over and over, but resist change because it threatens to destroy their identity. They are deadly in a DO. Serial incompetents, by the same token, are employees who could become competent in the usual sense, but instead regularly choose to experience temporary periods of incompetence, treating them as essential investments in staying one step ahead in an ever-changing world. A DO needs and needs to nurture serial incompetents. This involves making heavy investments in cutting-edge training and development, as well as providing unwavering support for employees who move from opportunity to opportunity in pursuit of smart risks that sometimes pay off in a processes in a way that actively encourages and facilitates ongoing workforce alignment. The two key sub-principles are:

- create a common cause
- embed contextual clarity.

The creation of a common cause requires the articulation of a[redacted] organizational vision[redacted]r mission that is both aspirational and inspirational – as Google has done with its well-known mantra 'To organize the world's knowledge' – and then clearly communicating it over and over in many different ways. The idea is to keep employees focused and fired up by making it perfectly clear what the firm exists to do and why this is a good thing for it, them and society. But employees also need to know where they fit in, which is why it is also essential to embed contextual clarity. This process begins with the articulation of the firm's business model(s) in a way that paints a complete picture of its environment, how it operates, what it takes for it to succeed and the crucial role that employees play in the grand scheme of things. It continues with efforts to assure that the business model is clearly understood and consensually internalized by all employees (potential techniques include surround communication, open-book management and commitment management – see Dyer and Shafer 2003; Galbraith et al. 2002).

Driven by a common cause and informed with contextual clarity, a DO's [redacted]ell positioned to [redacted]and the reasons behi[redacted] sudden changes [redacted] business plans an[redacted]o adapt accordingly[redacted]qually important, they [redacted]withal required to [redacted] environmental changes on their own, to use this information to make timely and appropriate adjustments in business plans or to instigate new ones and to do whatever they need to do to assure they are realigned with the new business situation.

Pursuing workforce fluidity

[redacted]orkforce fluidity is to assure that all employee moves [redacted] behavioural adjustments [redacted]hether they involve a single individual o[redacted]group of e[redacted]ssly and efficiently. A step in the ri[redacted]ecti[redacted]ys, is to do a good job of operationalizing the foregoin[redacted] princip[redacted]. Flexible planning [redacted]nd a shared minds[redacted]t grease the skids [redacted]f workforce transitions. B[redacted] this. Additiona[redacted] to the facilitation of external staffing (i.e., the addition and removal of people) and internal transitions.

Evidence suggests that firms often stumble when trying to use external staffing and internal transitions simultaneously (Anderson 2001; Brockner 1992; Charness and Levine 2002; Penrose 1959). In the small b[redacted]earlier this was indeed the case for firms operati[redacted]stable environments, [redacted]ut not for those operating in comparati[redacted]y dynamic environments [redacted]. Among the latter, holding the effects of [redacted]nt at high levels, firms that used both approaches concurrently increased their revenues by 34% annually, whereas those that shied away from this two-pronged approach had average annual revenue growth of about 20%. While hardly definitive, these data nonetheless suggest that for a DO the capacity to simultaneously employ external staffing and internal

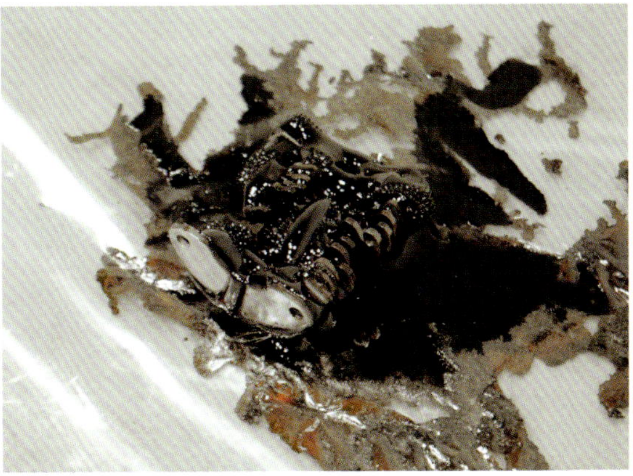
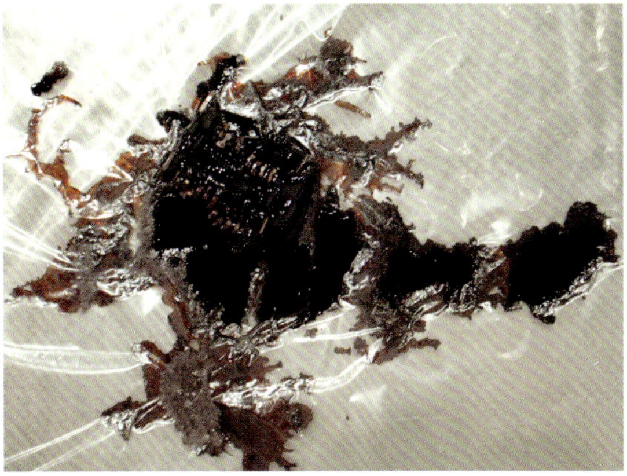

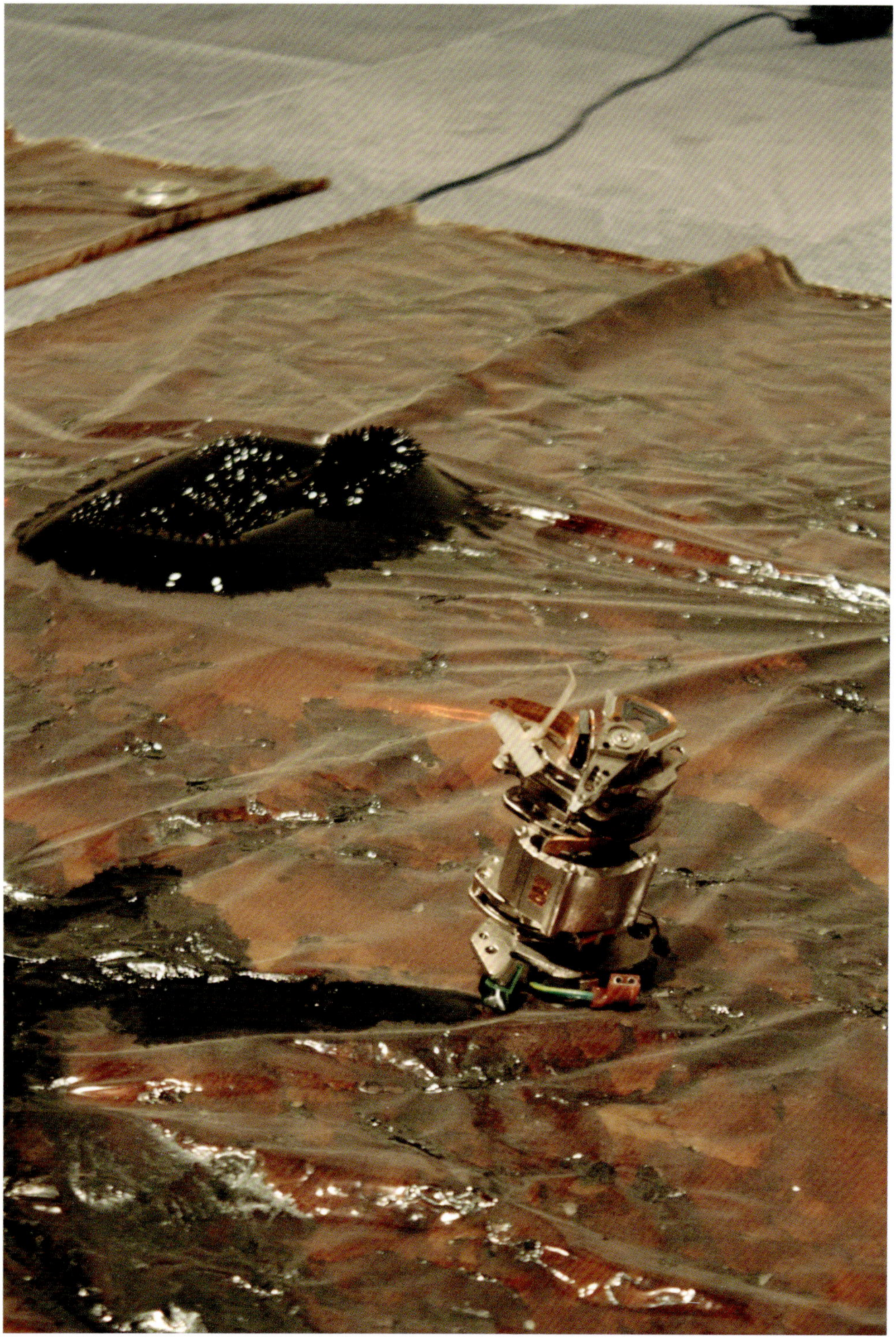

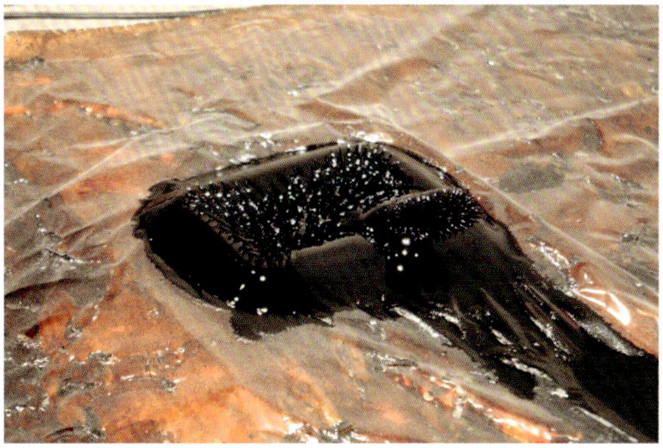

big way, but always result in highly valuable future-oriented learning even when they fail (McGregor 2006; Pascale et al. 2000: 250-57). Google's website again: 'There are hundred of challenges yet to solve . . . creative ideas matter here and are worth explo ing . . . [Googlers] . . . have the opportunity to develop innovative new products millions of people will find useful.'

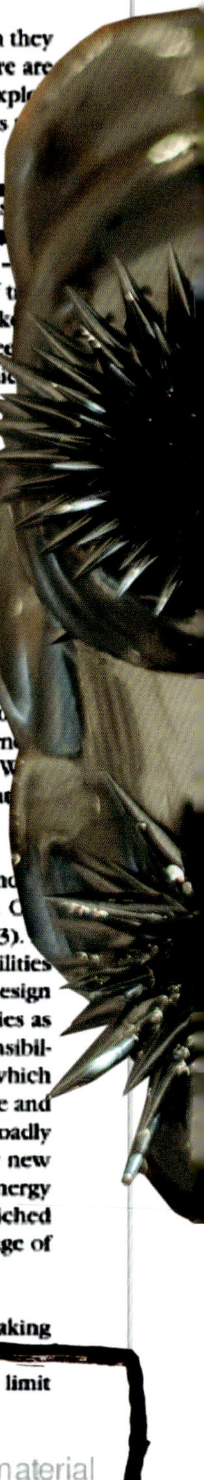

Facilitate interpersonal connectivity. Rapid redeployment [redacted] spontaneous laboration with ever-evolving groups [redacted] from facilitating interpersonal connectivity to build social capital – stock of meaningful relationships that foster and are fostered by high levels of t and cooperation among employees (Nahapiet and Ghoshal 1998) – which make easy for them to openly share information about where and when talent is ne and who does and does not possess the requisite competences and work ethic well as to dispense with preliminaries and get right to work when new tea formed. At Google, for example, there are hundreds of project teams, all with own websites to provide up-to-date information on the status and prospects ous ventures (Hamel 2006).

Of course, there is nothing easy about facilitating interpersonal conne Broadly, it involves (in addition to instilling a common mindset) breaking down that inhibit communication in typical organizations, such as beliefs that know power (and thus should be hoarded) and the formation of subcultures and while building up infrastructures that facilitate communication, such as smal (see Gladwell 2000: Chapter 5), communities of practice, open-plan offices 2000; Conlin 2006) and state-of-the-art organizational intranets (Hyatt 2006). involves enhancing opportunities for small, rotating groups of employees to together on a social basis (e.g., at off-site training programmes or even Friday aftern 'beer busts' of the type popularized in Silicon Valley). Or as Google puts is, 'W and play are not mutually exclusive. It is possible to code and pass the puck at same time.'

Expand [redacted]le orientations. Opportunity (O) in a DO stems in part from expand [redacted]tions so that few, if any assignments or tasks seem out of bounds. O way to do this is through discretionary-based work design (Dyer and Shafer 2003). most organizations, jobs are defined in terms of a litany of tasks and responsibilities and the ubiquitous add-on 'other duties as assigned'. Discretionary-based work design is quite different. Instead of 'other duties as assigned', it emphasizes 'other duties as assumed'. That is, it specifies only a minimal core of required tasks and responsibilities and then opens up a maximally expansive zone of discretion within which employees are expected to take initiative in determining what needs to be done and then finding ways to get it done. Employees are thus encouraged to think broadly about the organization and their work and to be constantly on the lookout for new challenges, as well as new ways of accomplishing familiar tasks. There is synergy here; expanded role orientations help to enrich the talent pool even as an enriched talent pool (imbued with a shared mindset) is ideally suited to take full advantage of expanded role orientations.

Unleash the talent pool. Exp[redacted]tions focus primarily on making adjustments without employee[redacted]changing roles[redacted] the realm of opportunity (O) f[redacted]crushing the constraints that limit

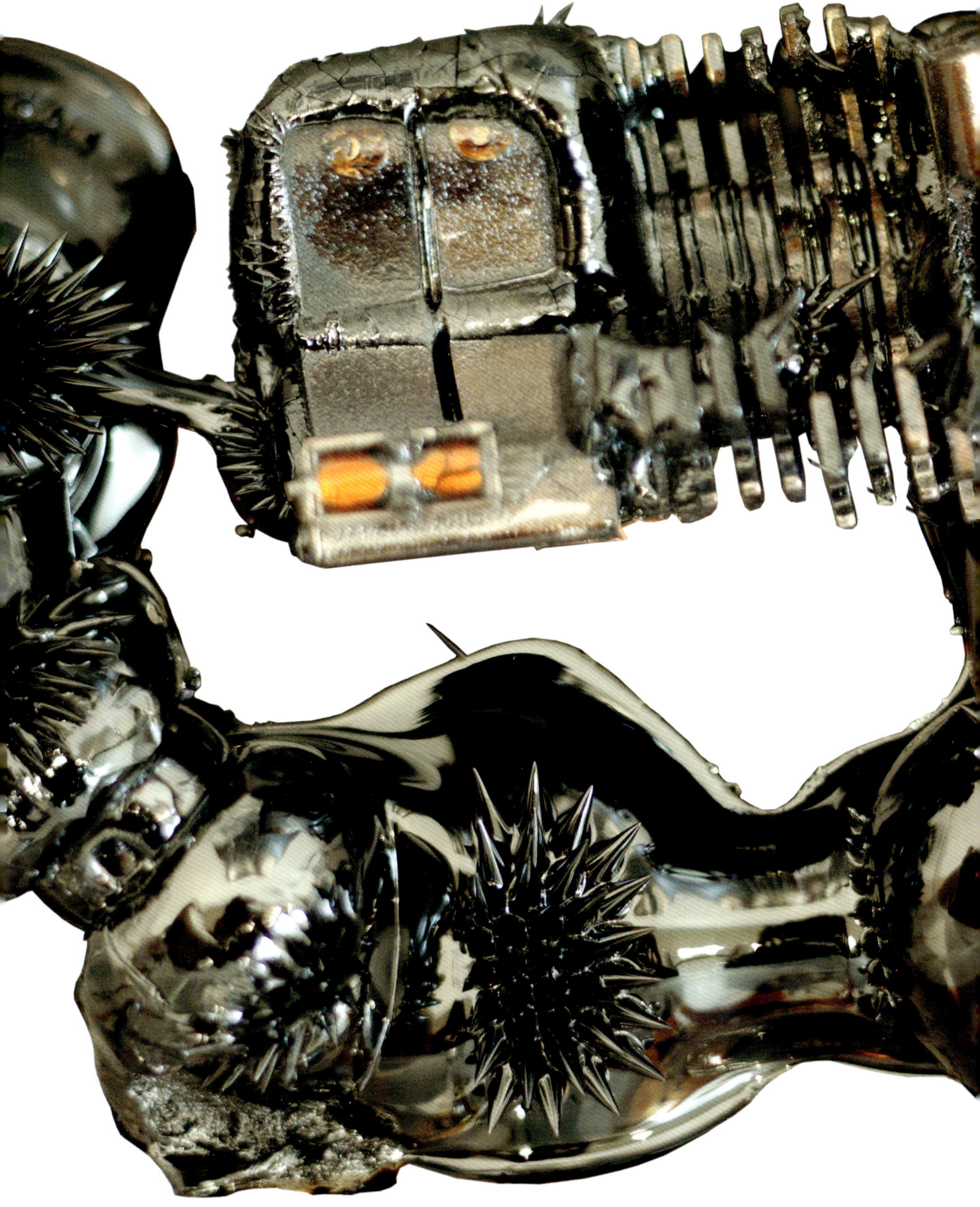

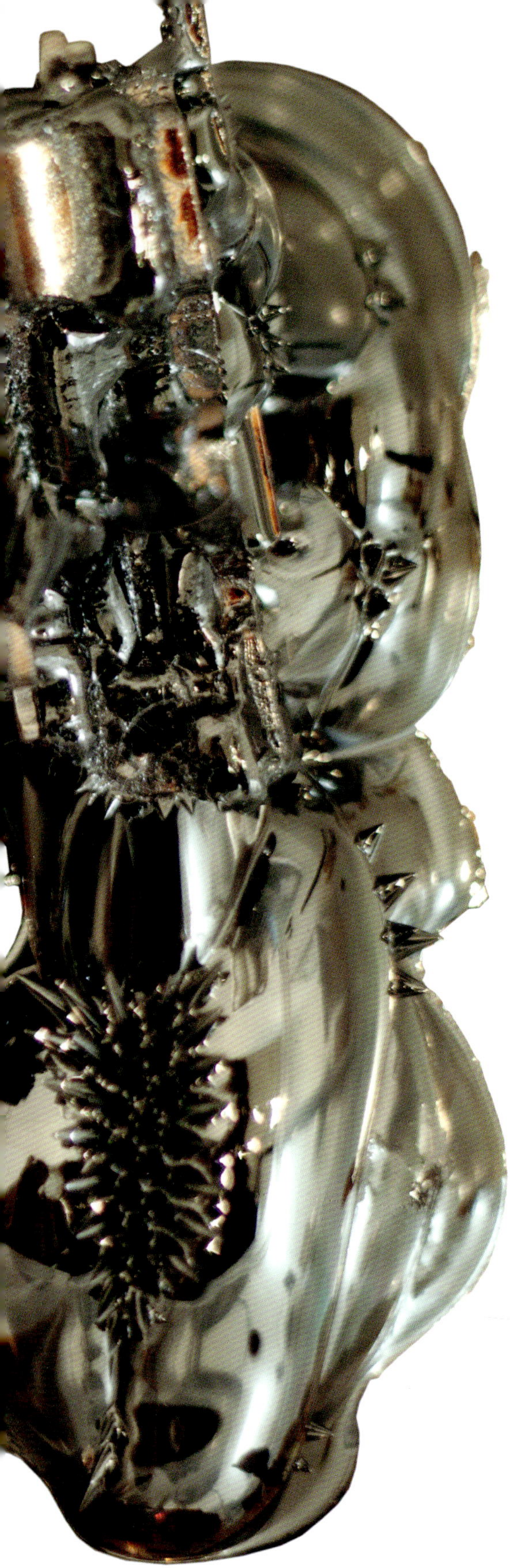

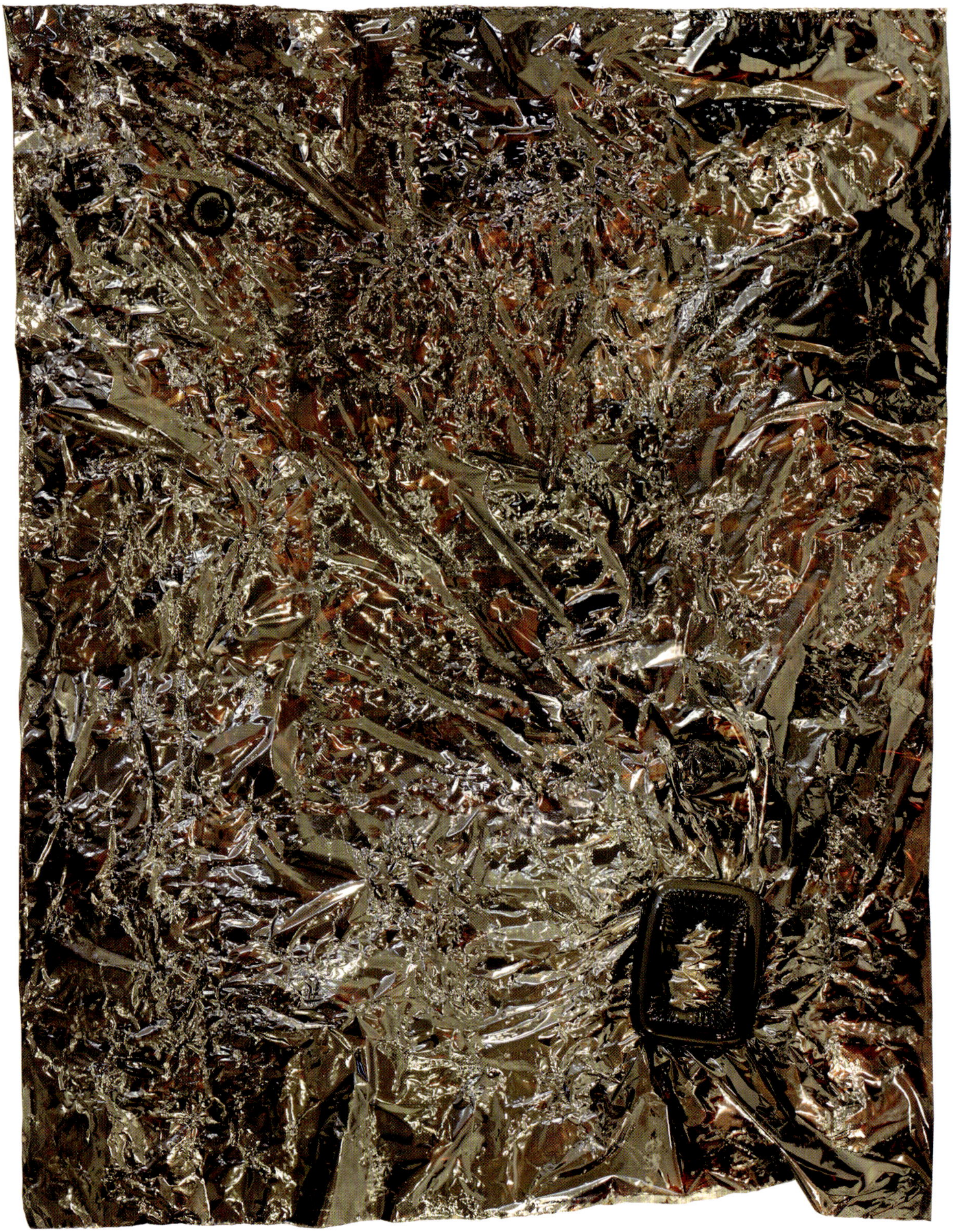

FLUID EMPLOYMENT

FULLY AUTOMATIC WRITING

Alex Kitnick

A woman is standing in early twentieth-century contrapposto, which is like the classical kind except with more torque and twist. Her left leg is kicked out over her right, her right arm is extended away from her torso, and her left arm is bent at the elbow with her fingers pointing at and barely grazing her head. It looks as if she might be performing a dance move or simply striking a glamorous pose. Her body is delicately draped in fabric with the same print on both her headscarf and dress. This way she is not all angles and edges but swoops and catenaries as well. The cumulative effect of these moves is a sense of grace and poise that seems rather distant from us today. The woman, after all, is a silent movie starlet from a 1914 number of *Motion Picture Magazine*.

Next to her, just outside the photograph, on the paper on which the photograph is mounted, is the letter *T*. The woman's body is posed a bit like a *T* but not exactly, not to a T.[1] She is not a Model T, which only comes one way: black and mechanical. The pairing of body and letter here appears apocryphal, with the letter coming after the body. To reduce this woman to a *T*—especially to a printed one like this—is to separate and abstract her from all that is specific about her.[2] And yet this strange pedagogical aid—a section of Sam Lewitt's 2008 work *Portfolio (MGM)*, a compendium of pictures and letters—still teaches us something. It serves as a reminder that language is derived from the sensible world, that it was first acted out on the level of the body.

There is a connection between sense and sensibility, of course, but there is also one between sensibility and style. Another way of describing this woman, then, might be to say that she has style, and that her style—like a cursive letter—stands in contrast to type (as in the type of the *T*). Derived from the word *stylus*,[3] style comes before type, and it implies a sense of possession that type lacks: Someone *has* style, we say, but someone *is* a type. (Perhaps this has something to do with the fact that one

1. She is not giving a *T* like a cheerleader might. She could do a better T if she wanted, but we sense that this wasn't her intent.
2. Reducing her to a still from a "motion picture" might be said to have a similar effect.
3. Merriam-Webster defines a stylus as "an instrument for writing, marking, or incising: as an instrument used by the ancients in writing on clay or waxed tablets; a hard-pointed pen-shaped instrument for marking on stencils used in a reproducing machine; a needle; a cutting tool used to produce an original record groove during disc recording; a pen-shaped pointing device used for entering data (as positional information from a graphics tablet) into a computer." *Merriam-Webster's Collegiate Dictionary*, eleventh edition (Springfield: Merriam-Webster, 2009).

holds a stylus in one's hand, but that one only ever taps at an apparatus that makes type move.) If type is a lead letter striking down on paper, style is a cursive gesture winding its way over a sheet—or down the street. Style implies a sense of cultivation, of self-care, a flourish you come up with yourself. Style shows through when writing with a stylus, channeling the idiosyncrasies of the hand, as well as its grace and movements.[4] Style has no place when the transition to type gets under way. Type is not fluid but cast, regulated and regular, repetitious—again and again and again. But perhaps only when type was cast did we notice how whole subjectivities are embodied in technologies of writing, and that we also inscribe ourselves while writing everything else down.

Writing, of course, is only one branch of language. Written or not, language has its structures, its rules and regulations, and if we play in it, it is only to a certain degree—language always has the first and last words in the game. Though structured, with the transition from hand-written manuscripts to movable type, language assumed more and more of a legislative logic.[5] Spelling was standardized, and with it, rules and regulations became widespread. Marshall McLuhan referred to this new world as the *Gutenberg Galaxy*, a space of relations founded on order, visuality, and single-point perspective. For Michel Foucault, the letterset world was increasingly a space of recording and regulation as well.[6] If language emerged from us, with letterset writing, it slowly began to turn back on us, creating classifications and files, systems of ordering and numbering. Even as electronic technology has replaced mechanical systems in the last hundred or so years, these bureaucratic inventions have remained. In fact, they have intensified, creating an ever-proliferating number of barriers and codes that never even really need to print themselves out. Since the early 2000s, Lewitt has made it his project to tease out connections between technologies of writing and the subjects that inhabit them. It is significant that he embarked on this project at the moment the lived world pushed ever more fully toward the brink of digitalization, when writing entered a new stage—and a new subjectivity followed it into being.

Enlarged images of antiquated printing mechanisms—computer-generated chromagenic prints—help make the stakes of Lewitt's project clear.[7] Roman letters fastened tightly into place by corsets of wood give orders to and declare things at the viewer. "GEOMETRY FOR EVERYONE," one states. The letters composing the words, stood on their side and, like all type, appearing backward to the viewer, are separated by empty rectangular placeholders. Another work reads "FACE FORWARD," its letters also turned around and tilted ninety degrees, crunched between yet more

4. In *Portfolio (Monograms 2 of 2)*, 2008, one sees pieces of paper full of marks, tests, daubs, lines, and strips of ink. An accompanying drawing of a pen is rendered in that same ink. A monogram is the emblem of style.
5. Indeed, as McLuhan notes, the shift from oral to written communication had a similar effect. "The goose quill put an end to talk," McLuhan writes. "It abolished mystery; it gave architecture and towns; it brought roads and armies, bureaucracy." Marshall McLuhan, *The Medium is the Massage: An Inventory of Effects* (New York: Bantam Books, 1967), 48.
6. Michel Foucault, *The Order of Things* (New York: Random House, 1970).
7. If they are *chases*, are we on the run?

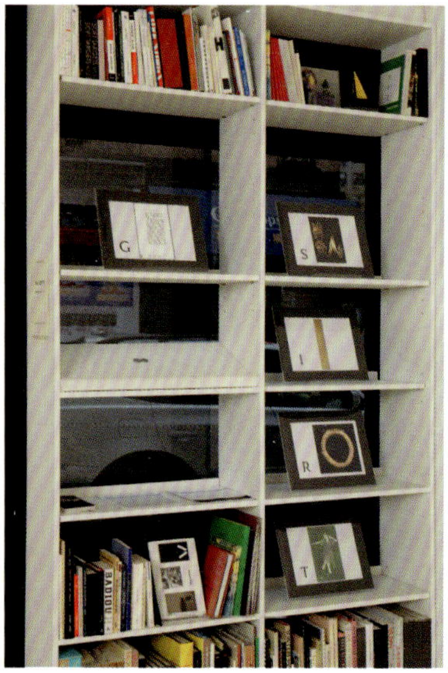

From top:

Portfolio (MGM), 2008 (detail)
Installation view Miguel Abreu Gallery, New York 2008
Five ink drawings on paper, color photocopy, book page, gold-painted segment of 35 mm film stock, postcard, two photographs, inkjet printout, archival museum board, all in plastic sleeves
Each 11 x 14 inches (28 x 35.6 cm)

Template: Recto, Verso, (4a/b), 2007
Screen print, collage, graphite
Sheet size: 25 ¼ x 34 ¼ inches (64 x 87cm)

Templates: sequence 10/.../10, 2010
Installation view Galerie Buchholz, Berlin 2011
Portfolio of ten screen prints on archival newsprint, inkjet on transparency of all watch ads from the *New York Times* October 2010, Mylar cover
Each 24 ⅘ x 33 9/10 inches (63 x 86 cm)

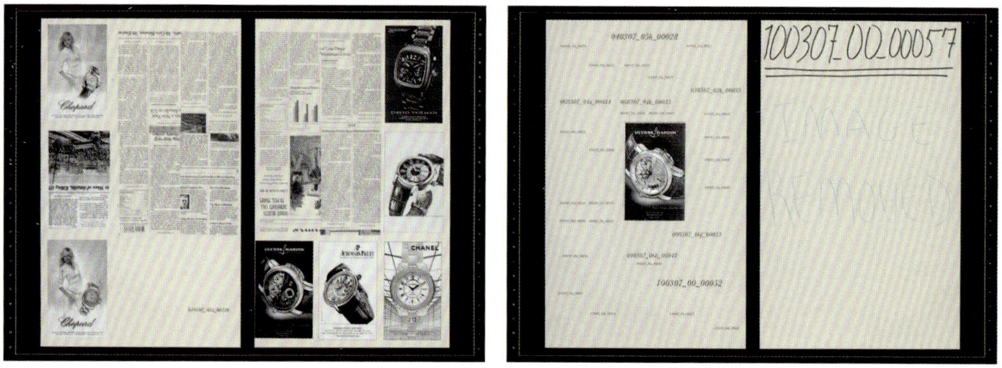

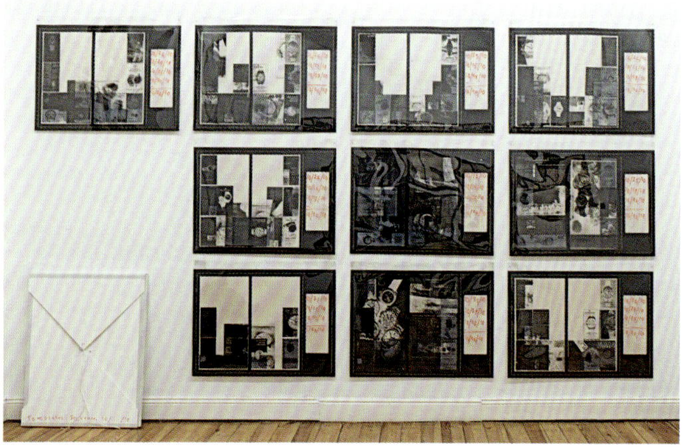

columns of hard-to-read text.[8] These pictures make printing mechanisms look like disciplinary devices; they have a kind of gallows humor about them. Rendered at human scale, the viewer has the sensation of literally being impressed upon by these works. They are letterpresses, after all: They press letters into place, but they also press letters onto people, press people into place. Yet, in their great detail—one can't help but notice the grain of wood and the rust of metal—they also endear themse-zlves to us, calling to mind a wonderful old contraption (or a particularly exciting fixture from Restoration Hardware). Surely, this has something to do with the amplification and magnification of detail going on within these works. One guesses that the original chases were smaller than this, more the size of a standard sheet of paper, though it's hard to know how big they were exactly. In the shift in scale these works enact, language appears both as a symbolic order and a literal one, marking and regulating its subjects. It is not for nothing that the artist calls these works *Paper Citizens*. Full of hard metal and devoid of paper, one figures that this title must apply to the viewer, pulped, flattened, and printed on as we are. If birth certificates, passports, and visas typically form the primary paperwork of citizenship, these works suggest that we too—as bodies—are also roped into the system. These works insist, quite literally, that people are broken up into types, and are typed upon in turn.[9] When I stand in front of these works (they seem to ask for a frontality that I want to turn away from), I think to myself: I am more multidimensional than that!

But the works, too, are more multidimensional than that. For all their relishing of analog technologies, their amplifying of the grain of wood and the patina of metal, they are also structured along the lines of the digital. Where many artists have recently paired analog with analog—one thinks of Tacita Dean's film of film, *Kodak*; or Zoe Leonard's dye-transfer prints of defunct TVs; or Moyra Davey's yellowing photographs of old stereo equipment—Lewitt re-pairs the analog with the digital, creating less of a confrontation or standoff between the two than a strange and disconcerting hybridization.[10] In *Paper Citizen 4327* and *Paper Citizen 01-12*, for example, this duality is brought out in full; various parts of the printing machine are suspended in midair, floating in a white field without backing, "liberated" from their stricture, no longer battened down. Indeed, *0110_Universal-City_1010* served as the title of one exhibition, at Galerie Daniel Buchholz in Berlin, which featured these works—a title that suggests a nonplace world, an everywhere, subjected to abstracting code.[11] There

8. I wonder if the viewer is meant to "read" these works. One could if one wanted to, but one would have to work hard and pay attention. It is almost impossible to decipher them when seen on a computer. In a recent article, "Media Specificities," in *Artforum* (September 2012), Pamela Lee writes some of these texts out for us. One says, "Automations must be able to learn from their experience and become more adaptive and communicative. The loop between the automation's perceptions and its actions must narrow on several levels of abstraction. The development of signal-to-symbol systems is integral to these challenges." These works require, or at least reveal differently to, a good reader.

9. Subcultures, for instance, respond to the categorization of people into types, through their emphasis on style. See Dick Hebdige, *Subculture: The Meaning of Style* (London: Routledge, 1979).

10. George Baker has written provocatively on this trio of artists. See, for example, "The Absent Photograph," in Moyra Davey, Speaker Receiver (Berlin: Sternberg Press, 2010), 53-99

11. The other exhibition that contained these works was titled *Total Immersion Environment*, a phrase that conjures up ideas of a 3-D mediascape, a first-person interactive shooter game.

is a tension in these works between the particularities of the material on the one hand (a materiality associated with the cast of type) and the abstracting lightness of digital manipulation on the other (a world that is fundamentally postliterate). It is a tension that challenges both the ecstasy of communication and the lure of nostalgia alike, delivering an image of the vexed forces that create our present day. We can't have one without the other, we see, the digital without the material; the two are deeply enmeshed. Hardware forms the substrate of a world of ever-expanding data, while immaterial networks generate physical forms. Everything solid does not simply melt into air. In fact, today, one might even reverse the equation. Humming with Wi-Fi and laced with carcinogens, air now gives us everything solid that we have in our world: FedExed sneakers, foreclosed homes, and cramped shoulders, among them.

Lewitt, of course, is not the first person to find himself in a universal city. George Grosz and John Heartfield landed there nearly a hundred years ago, in their Dadaist photomontage *Life and Activity in the Universal City at Five Past Twelve* (1919). Time was of the essence then, with everything happening all at once (even if again and again and again). Each minute counted: clocking in for work on time, finding your place on the line. Time is imagined as precise, without somehow being specific. Moments don't string together. Precise things happen in a homogenous time, without somehow being connected to the last. Nothing adds up. Fitting this logic, Grosz and Heartfield's world is a cacophonous space of sharp angles, shocks, and claims for one's attention; the exhortation of "Cheers, Boys, Cheer" appears next to car wheels, strips of film, and additional banners of (typed) text. The "medium" of the work fits this experience. It is what some have called a "typocollage" or a "typomontage," but it is perhaps more accurately a "gripping" "photoplay," even "a son of a gun," as the work itself suggests. Just a few years after Picasso's *papiers collés*, Grosz and Heartfield delivered an engineer's update on the form (derived from the German *montieren*, montage literally means "to mount, to assemble, to install"). The universal city for Grosz and Heartfield is one of overwhelming modernity, both seductive and sycophantic at once. It is spiraling and whirring and cutting. Grosz's clenched, creaturely figures barely seem to make it through Heartfield's cornucopia of catcalls, catchphrases, and camerawork alive.

It is Lewitt's innovation to turn this preoccupation with regulated time (one might even call it "typed time") into the basic makeup of digital code, to follow this modernity into its post- or hyper- phase. In his 2007 exhibition, *1010 in University City*, at Galeria Franco Soffiantino in Turin, the artist took a first step in this direction by pairing watch ads clipped from the *New York Times* (their hands always balanced at ten past ten: an open embrace, a dented smile) with an archival numbering system based on the file names of JPEGs. All of this information was mounted on newspaper paste-up boards, the site of another type of montage.[12] The newspaper, too, is a fundamentally temporal medium, with all of its far-flung stories united by a dateline (this phenomenon, however, seems on the brink of vanishing today with the advent of online editions in which each day is no longer distinct but rather permutes and

12. In certain works, hand drawings of old printing presses were also featured.

fades into the next). Indeed, rather than time, Lewitt's second "universal city" is increasingly made and regulated by files. (If time is money, it is also condensed into images—and perhaps this is how we will begin measuring time in the future: in JPEGs, in TIFFs, in videos waiting to load; images no longer even have images, as the string of digits hovering in these works suggest.) There is more silent stillness in this second life than untrammeled noise. The grid—both the ground plan of modernist painting and the imperative of the modern urban scene—reemerges, laying down its tracks. It's not even that it creeps back, as much as it just hangs there, never having gone away. While Grosz and Heartfield's vision was ruthlessly contemporary to its moment, exploding in all directions, communicating what it might have *felt* like to live at that moment by channeling its effects, Lewitt's rendering verges on, or at least evokes, obsolescence. It is not what our present feels like, nor even what it looks like. These works are less about feeling than they are about revealing, peeling back walls of hot graphics to show skeletal architectures beneath. They don't mime the present as much as look at it askance, revealing something of its infrastructure. They take an odd angle on our moment, perhaps delivering a prehistory, and yet, at the same time, the present moment is emphatically there in them, emphatically here. Indeed, where Grosz and Heartfield studded their scene with movie actors, Lewitt has included his own cast of characters. His *Cast List for Universal City* lists a litany of occupations written on the cardboard packaging of an "involving" Apple monitor, including "Late Workers," "Young Artists," "Pliant Staff," "Consumers," "Prosumers," and "Sad Designers" among its denizens. Their names are more or less interchangeable. All of them are characterized by malleability, and there is a fluidity between them. The Apple vortex universe pulls them all into the same miasmic whole.

These are the occupations that take place in the new field of writing, which might also be called the new field of automatic writing. Where the surrealists imagined automatic writing as something that would bypass the authority and intentionality of the author, break through psychic layers, and bring things to the surface that had otherwise been submerged, today there is a new kind of automatic writing (and also perhaps a new *underneath*). "Nowadays . . . manmade writing passes . . . through microscopically written inscriptions, which, in contrast to all historical writing tools, are able to read and write by themselves," writes Friedrich Kittler in his essay "There is No Software," a title that resonates with Lewitt's own interest in hardware.[13]

> The last historical act of writing may well have been the moment when, in the early seventies, the Intel engineers laid out some dozen square meters of blueprint paper (64 square meters in the case of the later 8086) in order to design the hardware architecture of their first integrated microprocessor. . . . Programming languages have eroded the monopoly of ordinary language and grown into a new hierarchy of their own.[14]

13. Friedrich Kittler, "There is No Software," *Literature, Media, Information Systems: Essays*, ed. John Johnston (Amsterdam: G+B Arts International, 1997), 147.

14. Ibid., 147–8.

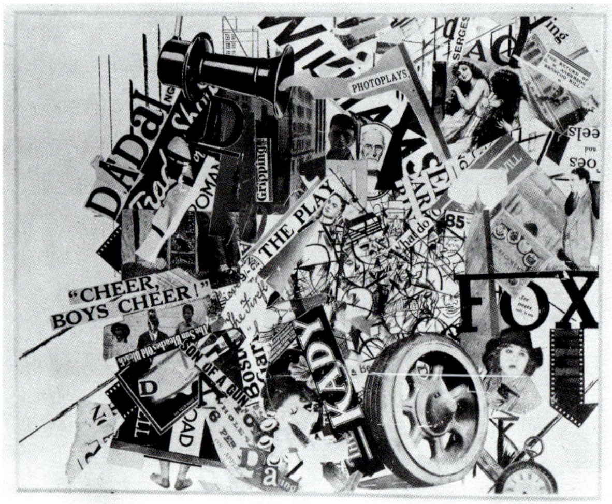

Clockwise from top left:

Georg Grosz and John Heartfield
Life and Times in Universal City at 12:05 Noon [Leben und Treiben in Universal City, 12 Uhr mittags], 1919
Collage, reproduction, whereabouts of original unknown

Cast list for Universal-City, 2011
Cardboard, marker
29.5 x 23.6 inches (75 x 60 cm)

Portfolio (Monograms 2 of 2), 2008
Portfolio with ink and graphite on paper, ink on paper, carbon paper, 4 x 5 inch negative in plastic sleeve, three color photocopies
Portfolio: 17 x 22 inches (43.1 x 56 cm)
Plinth: H 34 x W 35 x D 22 inches (H 86.4 x W 89 x D 56 cm)

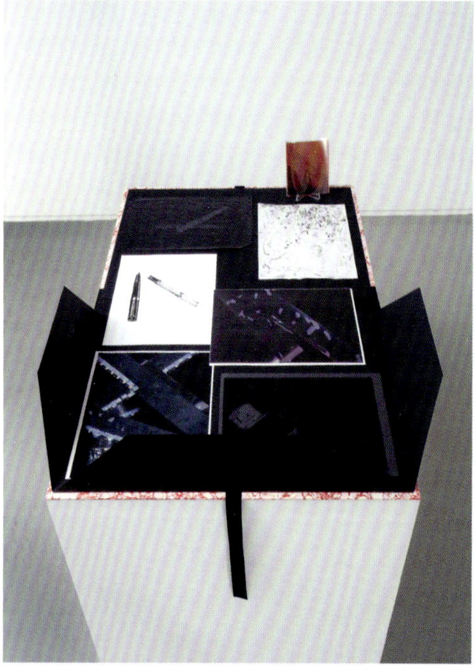

The computer puts an end to writing as we know it, Kittler claims; writing now writes itself, automatically, without a subject. As a result, language becomes autonomous, creating a language that doesn't need us, but that nevertheless compels us and moves us around with its numbers and code. We become its material. As the scene of writing gets smaller and smaller, deeper and deeper into the circuits, we have an increasingly difficult chance of fitting into it, of taking control of it to say something. At the same time, of course, we write more and more than ever before. When everyone can be a writer (and a publisher), Kittler surmises, writing dies—though perhaps it is more accurate to say that it splits in two. On the one hand, there is the computer's "automatic" writing, and on the other hand there is our own "automatic" writing—all of our texts and feelings and updates, constantly gushing forth as if they were programmed. There are two kinds of automatic writing now, but they weave back and forth, merging in and out of each other. Perhaps they are not as different as they first appear. The one feeds the other, each making the other possible. This is the new development in the history of writing. After style and type comes the language of the program. One might call it fully automatic writing.

One wonders sometimes if there is anything outside of language, not necessarily before it, but rather underneath it: a subtext of text; the thing that makes language run, that keeps everything together, that keeps the program going. The surrealists referred to this force as the unconscious, but today something more material comes to mind. To be very literal, to be incredibly bloody-minded, ferrofluid, a viscous liquid holding microparticles of iron in suspension, might be one thing that keeps the program moving. Lewitt calls it "an agent that moves in between other agents: it maintains and supports relations, it mediates their functionality."[15] Typically it slides into everything from microprocessors to stereo speakers, locked tight in a plastic casing or metal shell. In Lewitt's *Fluid Employment*, however, ferrofluid flows and twitches over a landscape of hard drives and credit cards, shimmered by plastic fans in open air, underneath gallery lights. Moving away from the vertical wall-bound work he is best known for (such as the *Paper Citizens*), Lewitt makes a horizontal move to the ground here, laying everything low. I think this work is meant to offer a kind of close-up view of life today, but it's a close-up that is also a wide-angle landscape: a new vision. When looking at *Fluid Employment*, one could be flying over the oil refineries of New Jersey, or have one's head stuck inside a computer terminal. One is behind the scenes and over the scene at the same time.

Like a lot of things today, *Fluid Employment* is not sustainable; it's not the kind of artwork that will endure for all time. When it was shown at the *Whitney Biennial* in 2012 (and who knows how or when it will be shown again), the artist made biweekly visits to the museum to replenish it, pouring fresh fluid over the desiccating stuff crystallizing on the machines. (In the *Whitney Biennial* catalog, Lewitt implicates himself in this material, showing us a picture of the artist's ferroreflection.) If he had not shown up, the ferrofluid would have hardened and turned into so much dense,

15. From an unpublished text by the artist.

dare I say *sculptural*, matter.[16] "Prolonged exposure to open-air circulation causes evaporation to occur at accelerated rates," a sign accompanying the installation warned. This tension between hardening and loosening is central to the work: Even though the artist hydrates, he is less that which makes it fluid than a part of the fluid system itself. He is a bit of the irrigation system, a little sprinkler servicing the work. If the model of artist as service sector employee has a long history by now, Lewitt mimes this position to new and disquieting ends. His services make the present look past, showing the scaffolding behind our current moment. What Theodor Adorno once said of Walter Benjamin might be said of the artist here as well: "He is driven not merely to awaken congealed life in petrified objects—as in allegory—but also to scrutinize living things so that they present themselves as being ancient, 'Ur-historical,' and abruptly release their significance."[17] By bringing our contemporary moment up to the brink of fossilization, Lewitt allows us to see it with distance. He shows us our moment as it might readily appear in the not-so-distant future.

But before we fast-forward, first rewind. In 1955, the critic Georges Limbour wrote a text on Jean Dubuffet titled "Let the Material Speak for Itself," in which he insisted that Dubuffet's art was less an exploration of form than an investigation of matter, a new kind of materialism. [18] In playing with matter, Dubuffet allowed different aspects of it to become visible. "It is matter in the same way as the world is matter," Limbour wrote, "and by plumbing the depths of this pictorial substance, analyzing it, transforming it, transmuting it, one can establish a link with the matter and the spirit of the universe."[19] Increasingly, Lewitt's work has taken a similar turn toward material, in an attempt (which might at first sound paradoxical) to articulate the immaterialities of our current age, to show its spirit, to give spirit form. Unlike Dubuffet, however, Lewitt does not attempt cosmic comprehension. Rather, he attempts to capture another spirit in his work, perhaps something along the lines of what Luc Boltanski and Eve Chiapello have called the *New Spirit of Capitalism*.[20] It is a spirit that is compelled to be fluid, but which also twitches and tends to evaporate. Like all spirits, it's invisible until it inhabits a body. Today it is transforming the working body (the whole cast of characters) into something unlike anything it has ever been before. We might call it a programmed body, the subject of a fully automatic writing. Time to edit, reprogram, rewrite.

16. Indeed, as Pamela Lee recently suggested, Lewitt's work might be a new kind of kinetic sculpture, though I think it is closer perhaps to the systems work of Hans Haacke than the meta-matic contraptions of Jean Tinguely. See Lee, "Media Specificities," 403–7.
17. Theodor Adorno, "Über Walter Benjamin," quoted in Michael Taussig, *Mimesis and Alterity: A Particular History of the Senses* (London: Routledge, 2002).
18. Georges Limbour, "Let the Material Speak for Itself," *Jean Dubuffet* (London: ICA, 1955), unpaginated.
19. Ibid.
20. Luc Boltanski and Eve Chiapello, *The New Spirit of Capitalism* (New York: Verso Books, 2007).

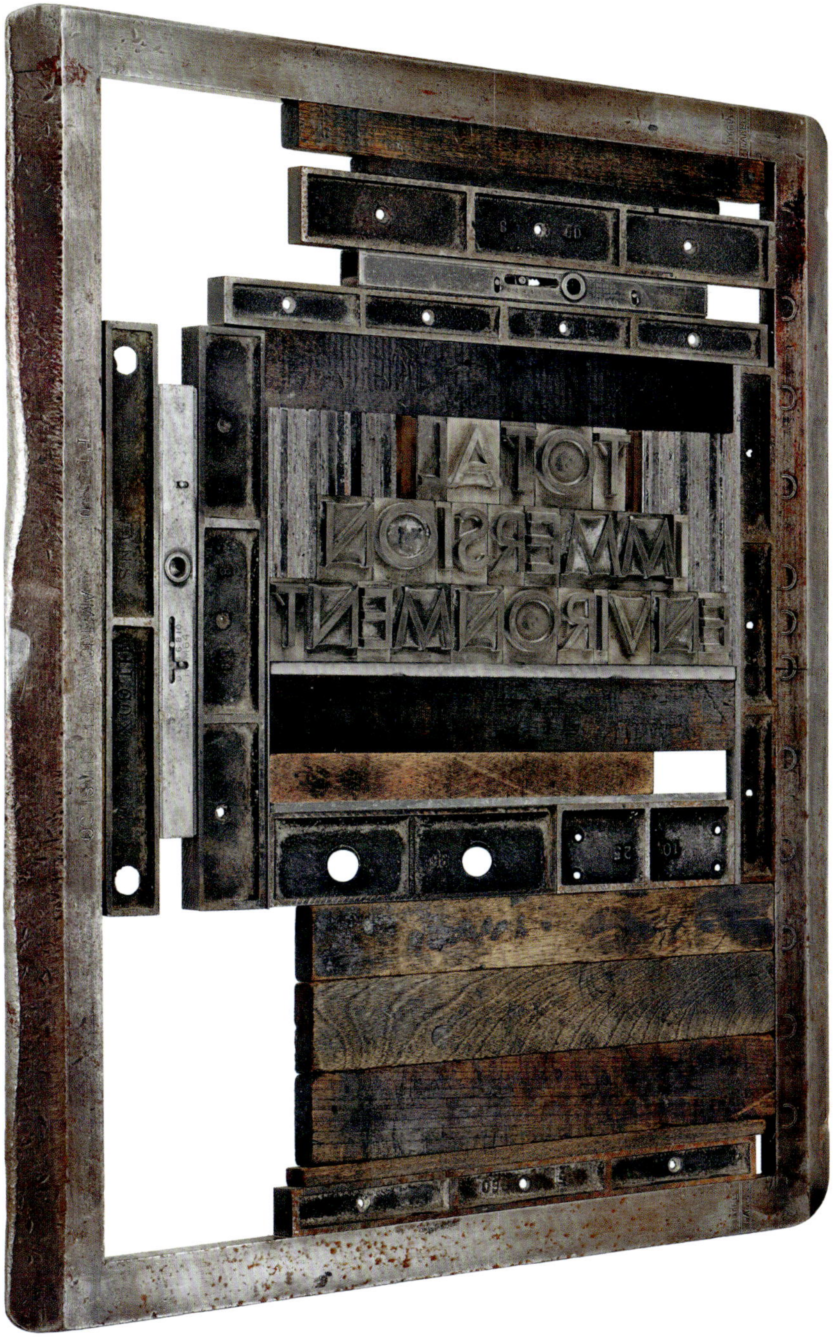
TOTAL
IMMERSION
ENVIRONMENT

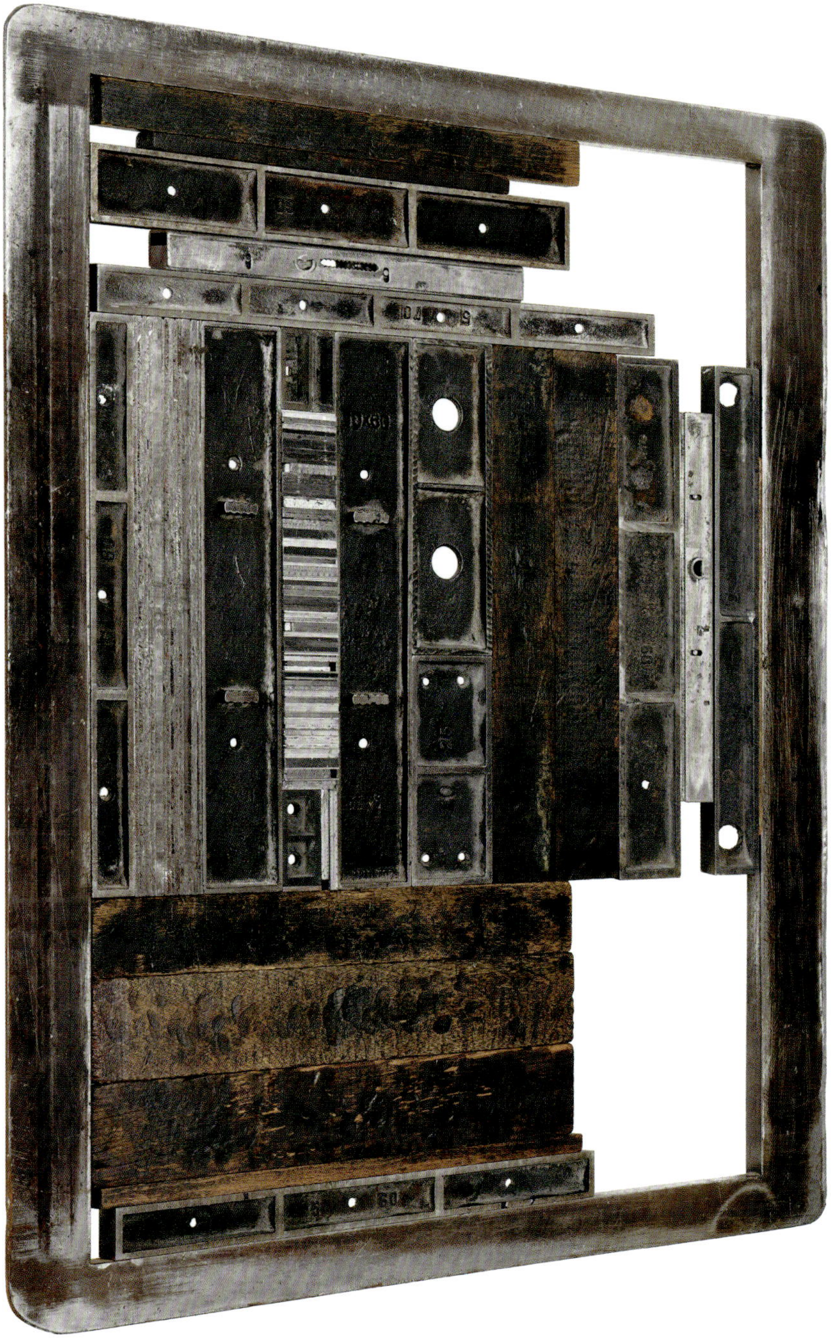

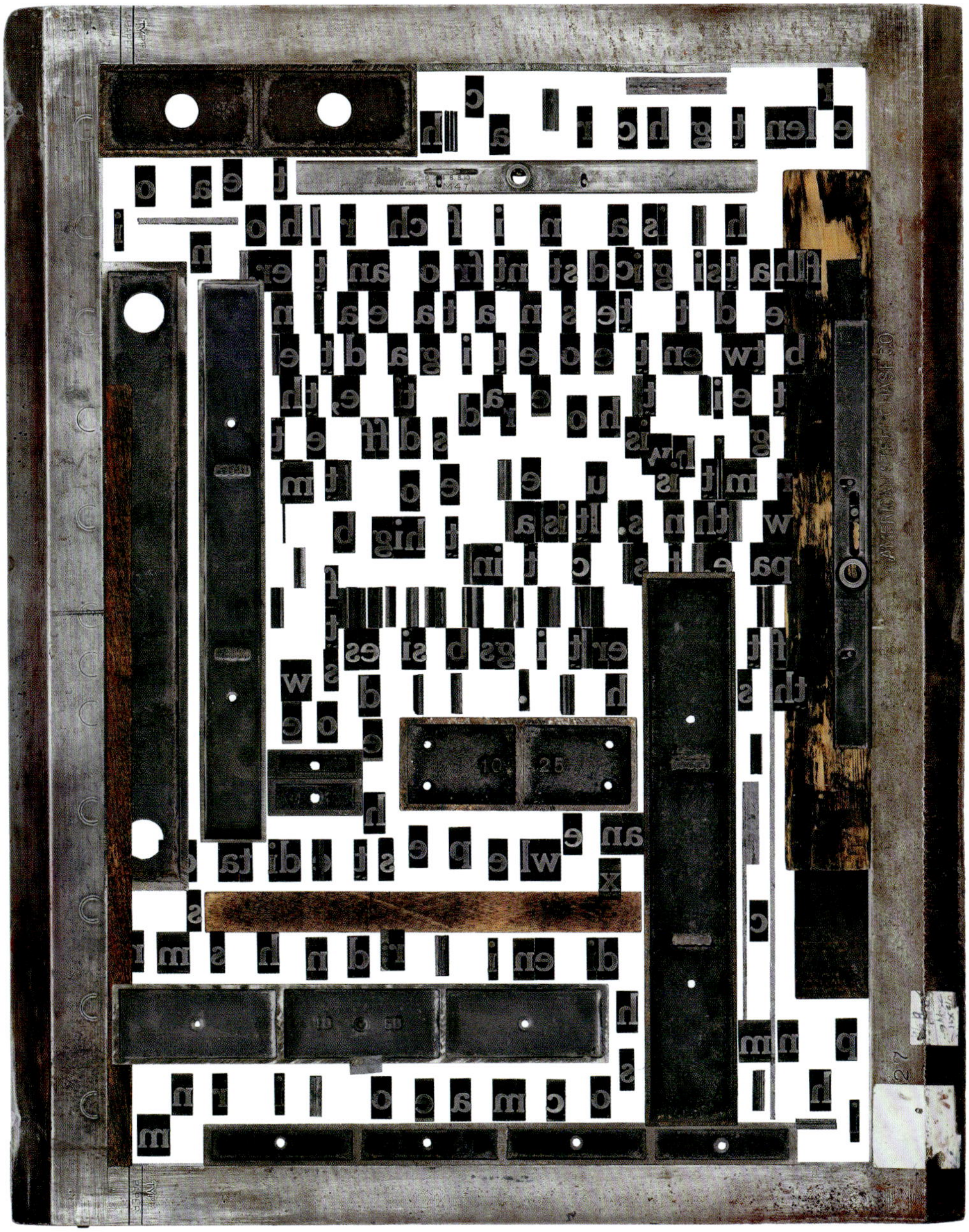

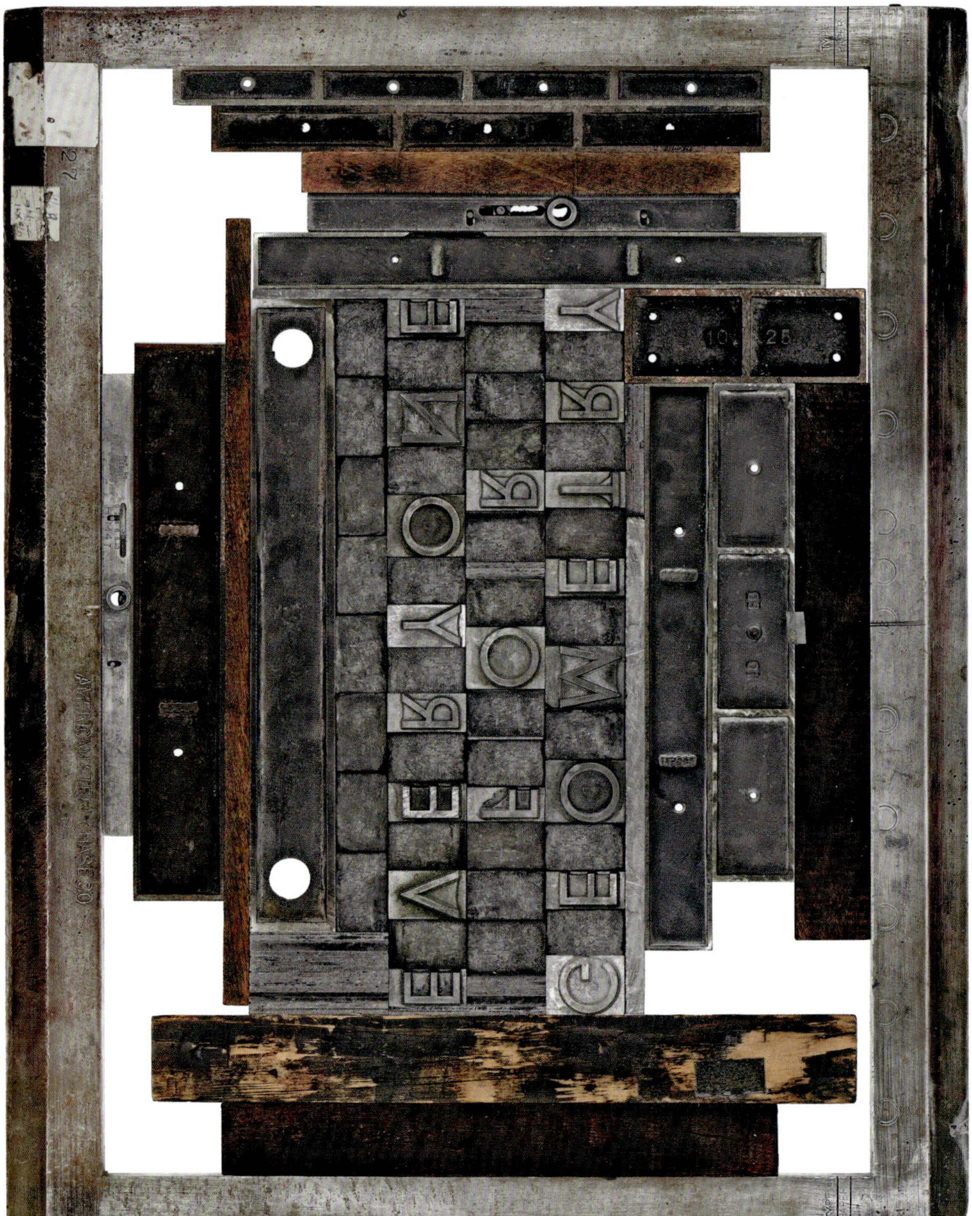

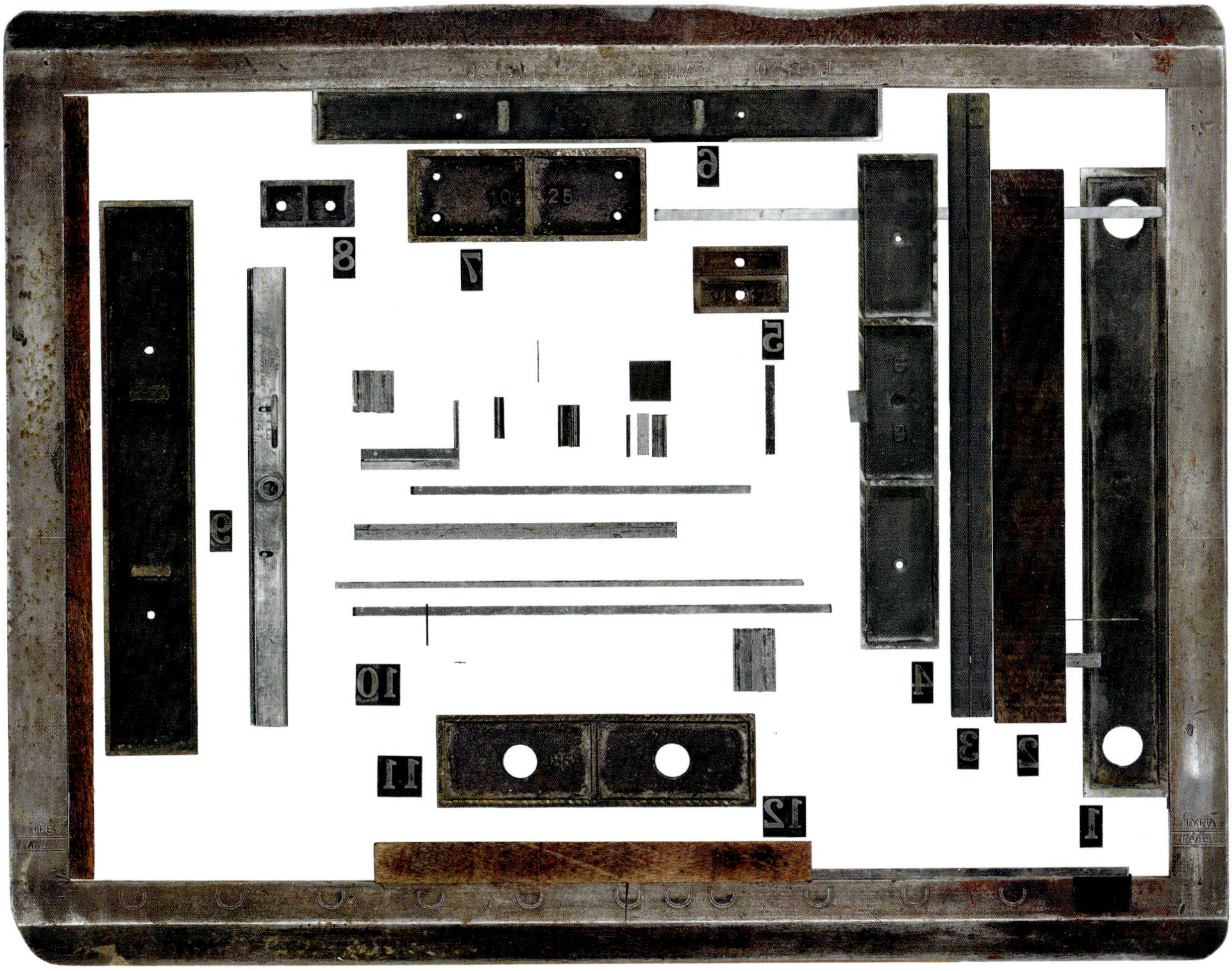

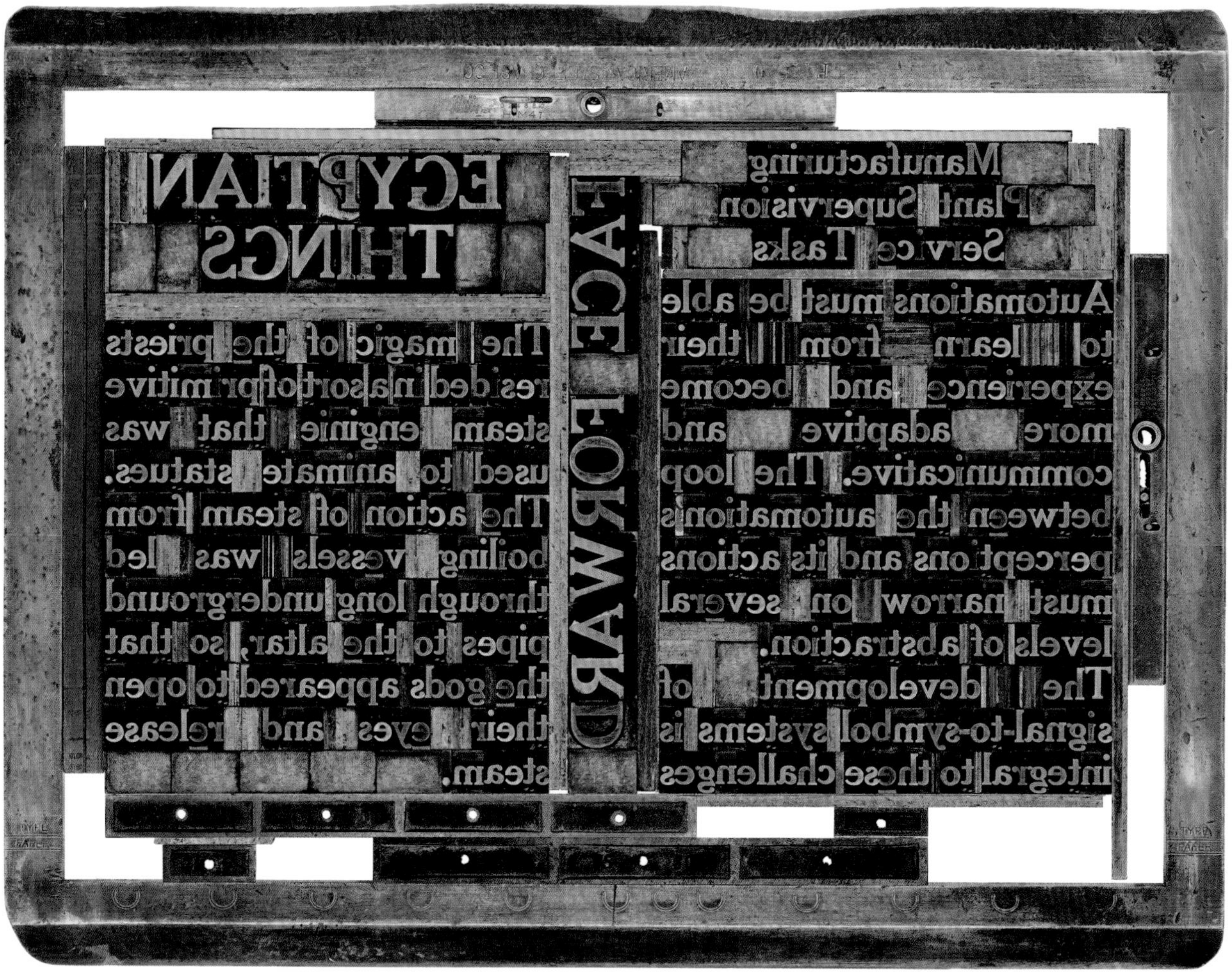
EGYPTIAN
THINGS
The magic of the priests
resided in a sort of primitive
steam engine that was
used to animate statues.
The action of steam from
boiling vessels was led
through long underground
pipes to the altar, so that
the gods appeared to open
their eyes and release
steam.
FACE FORWARD
Manufacturing
Plant Supervision
Service Tasks
Automations must be able
to learn from their
experience and become
more adaptive and
communicative. The loop
between the automation's
perceptions and its actions
must narrow on several
levels of abstraction.
The development of
signal-to-symbol systems is
integral to these challenges.

FRAMING MODERNITY: SAM LEWITT'S AESTHETICS OF SATURATION

Nathan Brown

> To take an attitude of partisanship towards key struggles of the past does not mean either choosing sides, or seeking to harmonize irreconcilable differences. In such extinct yet still virulent intellectual conflicts, the fundamental contradiction is between history itself and the conceptual apparatus which, seeking to grasp its realities, only succeeds in reproducing their discord within itself in the form of an enigma for thought, an aporia. It is to this aporia that we must hold, which contains within its structure the crux of a history beyond which we have not yet passed.
>
> —Fredric Jameson

In 2011, a show titled *Total Immersion Environment*, featuring large, high-resolution, composite digital photographs of antique letterpress plates. In 2012, a contribution to the *Whitney Biennial* titled *Fluid Employment*, exploring the physical properties and ideological imbrications of ferrofluid, a magnetic liquid used in a variety of military, industrial, and commercial electronic applications (hard drives, headphones, hydraulic systems, biomedical applications, military optics, paint on stealth bombers). If all art is concerned, in one way or another, with the relation between matter and form, this work is concerned with the mediation of that relation by technics. More specifically, it is concerned with (1) the immersion of this technical mediation between matter and form in what Foucault terms "discourse" (not only language or representations but the historically specific regulative apparatuses through which relations between words and things are produced and configured); and (2) the manner in which, within this immersion, the technical mediation between matter and form itself becomes a condition of possibility for historically specific discursive operations—for a discursive field, or what Friedrich Kittler calls a discourse network.

•

Let me posit a term for the point at which a practice of mimesis—immersed in the discursive immersion of the technical mediation between matter and form, yet cognizant of the power of this mediation to reciprocally constitute discursive conditions—renders this situation in a manner that undoes the distinction between matter and form or words and things (or better, renders the immersion of the work within the technical undoing of this distinction). We could call this saturation. The term designates a mode in which the handling of the complex of problems that I have been describing is not reflexive, nor minimal, not phenomenological, nor performative, nor "relational", but rather saturated: so replete with reflexivity that it is not reflexive but replete. Regardless of its precedents, I want to say that such an "aesthetics of saturation" only really has its place or comes into its own under specific historical conditions: our own.

•

Total Immersion Environment is gleaming, clean, precise—gridded floors and gridded photographs, meticulously recorded, composed, and presented.

The signal tension of these images is twofold and compound: between the process of their digital recording and the analog medium recorded; between the clarity of the photographs and the difficulty of decoding the texts that they present. This compound tension offers a clue to the manner in which the dialectical materialism of Lewitt's practice is also a historical materialism. The materiality of language in these photographs, which is also the materiality of the image, is mediated and transformed by the technological conditions under which its presentation is organized: "first" (historically), by the medium of the flatbed letterpress grid, then by the painstaking sequential work of frame-by-frame composite photography, digitally assembled and printed on paper; or, "first" (phenomenologically), encountered on paper by the viewer through the medium of a digital image whose subject is recognized and projected back into its media-historical context. Lewitt calls these images *Paper Citizens*. They show us the technical conditions of possibility for the emergence of the bourgeois public sphere. ("GEOMETRY FOR EVERYONE," one says.) But if, good members of imagined communities, we want to read the texts that these paper citizens present, we have to work backward, and therefore against the conventions of legibility encoded in the modern technology of the book.

Thus, the technical support of the book's production bears a reversal of its conditions of legibility. That this reversal—inscribed in the material substrate of technological production—is also, for us, a historical reversal, is implied by the digital capture of the analog mechanism. The retrojective effect of the former upon the latter is manifest in those images where the assembled linear continuum of the text fragments—pixelates—into discrete rectilinear components reminiscent of modernist geometrical abstraction.

Across the divide between the letterpress and the digital camera, we traverse mutations of art history within the history of the image. Framing this reversal and these mutations, leading us into if not through them, Lewitt is framing modernity—the technological conditions of its inauguration and of its end. But what do I mean by this last locution, "its end"?

•

Total Immersion Environment, 2011
Installation view Miguel Abreu Gallery,
New York 2011

0110_Universal-City_1010, 2011
Installation view Galerie Buchholz,
Berlin 2011

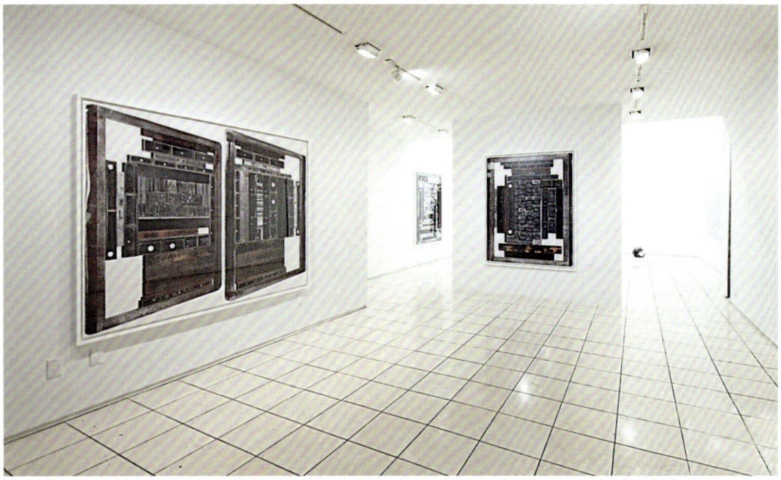

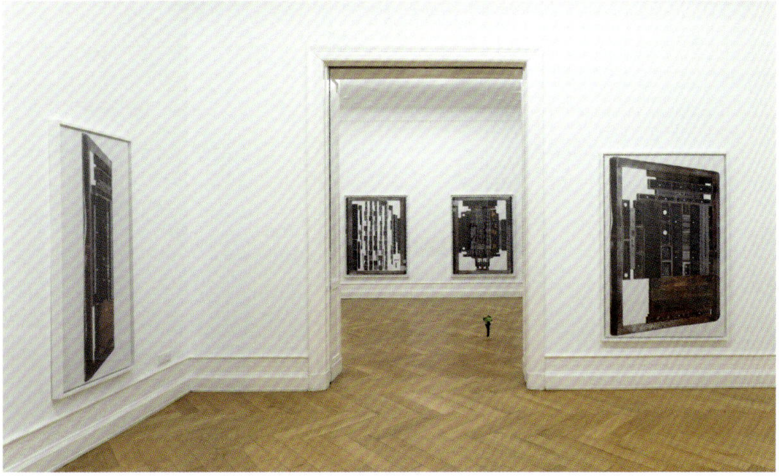

There is a curious misalignment of political-economic and cultural periodization in Fredric Jameson's title, *Postmodernism, or, The Cultural Logic of Late Capitalism*. The misalignment is between the "post" and the "late," the afterward of night and the nearly of evening. If we want to say that we indeed inhabit something like the time of late capitalism, perhaps we may also want to say that it is late in the day of modernity, but it is not yet night. From this perspective, the late modernism of late modernity would be the cultural logic of late capitalism, and the postmodernism of postmodernity would be the cultural logic of a postcapitalist mode of production and organization of social relations that has not yet come to pass. Postmodernism, not yet. Or rendered as a slogan: No postmodernism without postcapitalism!

Such a realignment of political-economic and cultural periodization would realign, also, the manner in which we conceptualize the relation between modernism and modernity, as well as the relation of the latter to "late modernity." Of course, modernity does not name a stable state of affairs but rather the process of modernization that has been theorized in terms of combined and uneven development. Late modernity, then, is the period during which this process is complete (never entirely, but in a structural sense): the time, for example, of the gradual and then precipitous structural integration of Russia, China, and India into a global economic system. The time, in other words, of so-called global capitalism, which Jameson aligns with postmodernity. He does so precisely because he thinks of modernity as a process of modernization that is (more or less structurally) complete. But if we want to say that the history of capitalism is congruent with that of modernity (recognizing all the historical contradictions that inhere within both), then we may want to reserve the term "late modernity" for the period of late capitalism during which both the development of global capitalism and the history of modernity arrive at their maturity, and thereby give us a sense of their ending—though they have not yet ended. Modernism, then, will designate a mode of cultural production within which modernity comes to deal reflexively (modern-ism) with the contradictions attendant upon its incipient maturity—contradictions that a properly Marxist periodization would recognize as part of the process of real subsumption. Thus we move, for example, from the eighteenth-century quarrel between the ancients and the moderns to the dialectical opposition of futurism and primitivism, within which the intensely lived contradictions of rational and technological "progress" are brought to the fore, as they are in the experience of and the cultural response to the First World War. It is the accomplishment of real subsumption, as the postwar boom of 1945–1965 draws to a close, that gives way onto what Debord calls the Spectacle, and it is the cultural logic of the Spectacle that I would identify as late modernism, or, the cultural logic of late modernity. This cultural logic includes those phenomena so perspicuously analyzed by Jameson, though their periodization is realigned: late modernism, late modernity, late capitalism. Such a realignment would not insist too much upon a sharp break between the cultural logic of the 1970s or 1980s and that of modernism proper—a break that has always been impossible to establish, except through efforts to hypostatize one or another aspect of modernism as representative of the whole (thus the desperate category of "high modernism"). Rather, it would situate the work of a figure like Warhol, for example, through the dialectical relation between technology, production, and the cultural function of the image that Warhol's work performs and expresses, not through a putative opposition to one or another strategy of modernist representation or abstraction. This historical materialist manner of periodization was the point, in the first place, of Jameson's cogent assertion that the veritable existence of something called "postmodernism" depends upon the existence of a recognizable postmodernity—that is, upon the historical situation of aesthetic criteria. In accepting the preestablished terminology of the "post," however, Jameson elided the consequences of his own important claim: that the cultural logic he was analyzing was that of late capitalism. These consequences, I argue, would follow from the recognition that something like a recognizable postmodernity is not yet upon us, precisely for the reason that late capitalism is not yet postcapitalism, and that the historical period and cultural logic of the latter have not yet come to pass.

This realignment confronts us with the problem of the future. Late modernity is that time when the maturation of modernity gives way onto the sense of an ending—a sense of nothing less than the end of capitalism, yet to come but drawing nigh. That the end of capitalism will mean the veritable end of modernity—of its mode of production and system of social relations (rather than simply its own ideological self-conception, its "grand narratives")—is a more daunting prospect than we might like to admit. That modernity will well and truly end means that the forms not only of thought and of culture, but also the forms of organization and the forms of life it has produced, will end with it. Shorn of communist teleology (though not of concrete communist measures), we do not know what will follow. Cyberpunk and science fiction, the exemplary narrative forms of the Jamesonian postmodern, are, for the most part, technological extrapolations of late capitalism and late modernity into the future. But the void future of postcapitalist life, of postmodernity as it presents itself to our own late modernity, is less like William Gibson's matrix than like the whale in Lászlo Krasznahorkai's *The Melancholy of Resistance*. Unlike Melville's whale, this one doesn't lead us on in the manic quest of manifest destiny, searching for the meaning of modernity. Rather, it is already dead: a vast, unassimilable, meaningless body laid out in the wagon of an obscure carnival presided over by a nihilist prince. At best, we can peer into one of its eyes and brood upon its enormity. Jameson is correct to say that it is easier to imagine the end of the world than the end of capitalism. But his famous remark is best applied to the late modernist problem of imagining the forms of organization and cultural production of a postmodernity we do not yet live, rather than to the representational impasses of a postmodernity we already inhabit.

•

At the 2012 *Whitney Biennial*, a rust-colored substance oozes across rectangular sheets of plastic laid on the floor, coagulating in spiky black blobs around magnets distributed unevenly beneath the surface, while microtowers of e-waste—hard drives, speaker components, and other little heaps of technological detritus—rise out of the goo like crumbling remnants of a drowned postindustrial city or grotesque extrusions from a sprawling toxic dump. This is what late modernity looks like as it draws to a close: saturated. Beside each plastic sheet, cheap plastic fans blow air across the surface, speeding evaporation.

On October 5, 2012, some four thousand workers at Foxconn factories in Zhengzhou, China, went on strike, refusing new quality control standards imposed for the production of the Apple corporation's marquee product, the iPhone 5. The largest manufacturer of electronic components in the world, Foxconn employs over one million workers who live in onsite complexes, usually hundreds or thousands of miles from their families. The lives of these workers bleed into the indistinction between the minutia of assembly-line labor and the tedium of existence in corporate factory-cities, with no exit from either. Under these conditions, the primary form of protest by Foxconn employees has been suicide, with workers taking their own lives at an alarming rate over the past several years in a terminal form of struggle. The corporation has responded by refusing life insurance payments to the families of employees whose deaths are deemed intentional. But this autumn, workers have channeled collective despair into collective resistance, rioting in September, striking in October, and beating the quality control staff who patrol assembly lines. "Factory management turned a deaf ear to complaints about these conflicts and took no corrective measures," reports China Labor Watch.

•

If, as Marx tells us, every product of labor is a social hieroglyphic, then every such product is also a material sign of the dialectical relation between the history of capitalism and the history of technology. In this sense, the production of consumer electronics at Foxconn might be taken to distill in its contemporary form the whole movement of the contradiction between capital and labor, from the industrial revolution, Taylorism, and Fordism, to the offshoring of manufacturing labor and the growth of the tertiary service sector, accompanied by the contemporary simultaneity of deindustrialization and post-Fordist labor with the persistence of the most traditional forms of miserable factory work. Information technologies are at once the result of and the condition of possibility for this last turn of the dialectical screw: The division of intellectual and manual labor between Cupertino and Zhengzhou gives the lie to the myth of "immaterial labor," even as the electronic devices produced in factories enable deindustrialization to continue apace. The explosion of unwaged surplus populations living in vast slums is as much the result of "technological progress" as is the submission of Taiwanese workers to impossible quality control standards or the geek utopia of corporate headquarters in Silicon Valley, powered by in-house Starbucks caffeine and yuppie commuter shuttles to San Francisco. Thus, the gleaming surface of the iPhone is the obverse side of the labor revolts to which the conditions of its production give rise. Both, in their mutual duplicity, bear all the contradictions of modernity within their discrepant manifestations. When we catch a glimpse of our reflection in the one, what we are looking at is our implication in the other—even if, Narcissus-like, we do not see it.

•

What *Fluid Employment* displays is something like the substance of this unseen, of what flows beneath the surface of the gadgets to which we pay too much attention—the substance of the electronic surfaces upon which we seem to live and breathe and have our being. The damaged life described by Adorno is now terminally dependent upon its Facebook respirator—at least in the circles frequented by the artists, intellectuals, celebrities, and tourists who make their way through the Whitney. In *Barbarism*, his scathing denunciation of technological modernity, Michel Henry follows Marx in observing that the process of production proceeds "in a state of affairs where life is absent and where it is never taken into consideration, either as a cause, an end, or even a means." "What then," he asks,

> is the state of affairs from which all production proceeds in the technological world, if this production has emptied praxis from itself and constantly seeks to do so, and if it is reduced to an objective process? It is the prior state of the instrumental network, that is, all of the technologies existing at the given moment. . . . Every new device and every technology is implied in some way by the system of existing technologies. They result from their interconnection and relationships. Whatever can be conceived and realized through them and whatever possibilities they contain will exist for sure. This invincible movement is called progress.

"Quality control" is the name of the managerial apparatus through which this invincible movement moves through the living bodies to which it is blind.

•

Along with its sheets of ferrofluid laid out across the floor, *Fluid Employment* includes a print encased in Mylar, assembling terms drawn from the website of a company called Ferro Tec: "magnetic," "silencing," "tumors," "computer," "efficiency," "separation," "Bio-medical," "trinkets," "domains," "sealing," "variable," "targeting," etc.

Lewitt describes ferrofluid as a substance that "continuously adjusts to changing contextual demands when sealed into a magnetically regulated environment, providing frictionless performance in an ever-widening range of applications, with minimal risk of evaporation." In an interview he notes the "strange collapse between the physical properties of the material and its ideological description": self-motivated, flexible, self-organizing, and so on. Indeed, the history of ferrofluid is concurrent with the emergence of a post-Fordist regime of accumulation whose managerial ethos has been described in the same terms. Discovered by NASA technicians in the 1960s, ferrofluid is a product of the Cold War, and its commercialization in 1968 corresponded with political revolts whose antiauthoritarian rhetoric had been anticipated by the technocratic fathers of the network society. Boltanski and Chiapello report that already in the 1960s, and in virtually all management texts of the 1990s, "we find advice on implementing the flexible, inventive organization that will be able to 'ride' all 'waves,' adapt to all the changes," so as to "secure a permanent technological advantage over competitors." At once a material component of consumer electronics and a physical synecdoche of the fluid employment they enable, ferrofluid is a dialectical substance. Like the movement of the Concept (or Capital), it is agitated by a restless negativity that sustains the becoming of its content, even as it undoes the forms that content becomes. Behaving as both a solid and a liquid, its capacity for self-organization derives from its "erratic structural traits"—a capacity for "continual modulation and recomposition." When its temperature rises, for example, ferrofluid becomes less magnetically sensitive, thus allowing cooler fluid to continually circulate toward magnetic fields situated near warm electronic components. On the basis of these properties, Apple has a patent for ferrofluid's use as a coolant. As Lewitt puts it, ferrofluid functions as a "liquid workforce"—one that never goes on strike, we might add.

•

But the 1990s (let alone the 1960s) were a long time ago. In the United States, the ideological babble of post-Fordist management did not prevent the tech bubble from popping. And several years after it popped, speculative markets spinning through the servers came down—first in the US, then in Europe, soon in China. Financialization, says Braudel, is a sign of autumn; it always attends the end of a world system. But though the seasons are cyclical, it has been hard to shake the feeling that the winter to come may freeze into an ice age, that the time may be out of joint, and that the far-off spring may bring with it not just a new global hegemon and another epoch of capital, but an altogether unknown weather. This is the feeling that modernity is saturated, that it did not end in the 1960s but it may be ending now, and that its end will be attended (halting, disjunctive, uneven) by the end of capitalism.

•

In the autumn prior to the riots of fall 2012 in Zhengzhou, Lewitt's time was split between preparing his contribution to the *Whitney Biennial* and participating in the daily life, material confrontations, and spectacular demonstrations of Occupy Wall Street in New York City. This, too, was an occasion for reflection upon the duplicitous dialectics of self-organization and their relation to the end of capitalism:

> *Fluid Employment* came together through reflecting on organizational forms relating to my work, and certain political groups that I and many others were involved in at the time.... The recurrence of the language of self-organization seemed tensely held between a desire for immediacy, and

> the medial language of the decaying managerial culture that serves as the backdrop for many of the people participating. The goal on some level was to consciously work from the position of unresolved contradictions saturating the conceptual tools mobilized in hope of transforming social relations. These conceptual tools are already circumscribed by the technical, organizational structure of the social environment in the present.

In an important 1977 analysis, Paul Mattick renders with particular lucidity the simple point that the history of proletarian struggles is structured by the history of the capitalist mode of production within which those struggles take place. The organization of struggles will inevitably bear within its forms and social relations the counterrevolutionary determinations of capitalist social relations. This means that the struggle to create new organizational forms is also a struggle against the organizational forms we create, since what these forms instantiate or "prefigure" is never only revolutionary but also counterrevolutionary. This is why we should never expect revolutionary groups and movements to be any less riven by contradiction than the social order within and against which they revolt. The moving contradiction between capital and labor inheres as much within the struggles of the latter as it does within the valorization of the former.

After the historical eclipse of the labor movement that organized struggles for 150 years, to recognize the intractable problem of organization that Mattick describes—rather than denying that it exists—is also to recognize the saturated condition of late modernity. The forms of the organized labor movement (the party, the union, the council) are modern forms of organization (government, bureaucracy, factory), and the ready-made structures they offered have now grown tired and obsolete—even as their structural contradictions still manifest themselves in the tension of general assemblies, working groups, affinity groups, anarchist milieus, and the separation of black blocs within marches. The unfolding of these contradictions in struggle is a matter of historical process, not of strategic lucidity and voluntaristic desire. Reformism, Mattick reminds us, requires a reformable capitalism, and this is what there one day will not be—not because we wait for that day to come but because we act within the medium of contradiction rather than the ideal of its projective resolution. This medium embodies what it only seems to figure, undoes the distance between what we say of it and what it is.

•

It is the saturation of modernity that bleeds out in *Fluid Employment*, pours onto the floor and evaporates, undoing the apparatus of distinction between matter and form, words and things, presenting this undoing not as matter of historical destiny, salvation, or catastrophe, but as a matter of historical fact.

FLUID EMPLOYMENT

MATERIAL HISTORY

Ferrofluid is a magnetic fluid technology. It first appeared on the technological scene in the 1960s when a researcher at NASA tried to create a magnetic rocket fuel that could be manipulated under zero gravity by powerful magnets and fed into rocket engines. This did not work. The fluid was subsequently licensed by NASA to AVCO Corporation and went straight into private research and development. Commercialization began in 1968.

Against the backdrop of late 60s social unrest in factories and schools, struggles against Imperialism and widespread opposition to top down systems of rigid authority emerged this eminently adaptable substance. Ferrofluid's self-organizing magnetic properties act like a liquid workforce. It continuously adjusts to changing contextual demands when sealed into a magnetically regulated environment, providing frictionless performance in an ever widening range of applications with minimal risk of evaporation.*

The exquisite pliancy of Ferrofluid is caused by its invisible, erratic structural traits. The liquid is composed of randomly circulating ferromagnetic nanoparticles whose time derivative is everywhere infinite (Brownian motion). When used in conjunction with a strong magnet the ferric nanoparticles take the shape of the magnetic field, creating localized clusters that appear to the eye as spiky globules which are capable of continual modulation and re-composition.

Many possible applications have been envisioned for Ferrofluid and more are still to come. Loudspeaker technology was one of the first and continues to be one of the largest market segments, going into over 300 million speakers each year at over 300 different companies. Employment of this material has branched out into diverse sectors of industrial production. Its uses range from military optics to biomedical research, from the paint mixture on the stealth bomber to sports car hydraulics, from domain detection for media such as magnetic stripes and disks to manufacturing systems in need of hermetic sealing, from classrooms to consumer electronics or simply as conversation pieces for the office or home.

* Prolonged exposure to open air circulation causes evaporation to occur at accelerated rates.

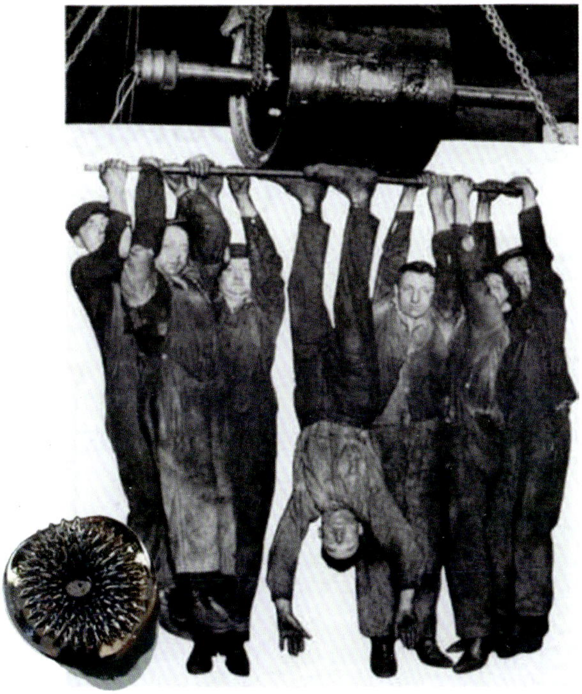

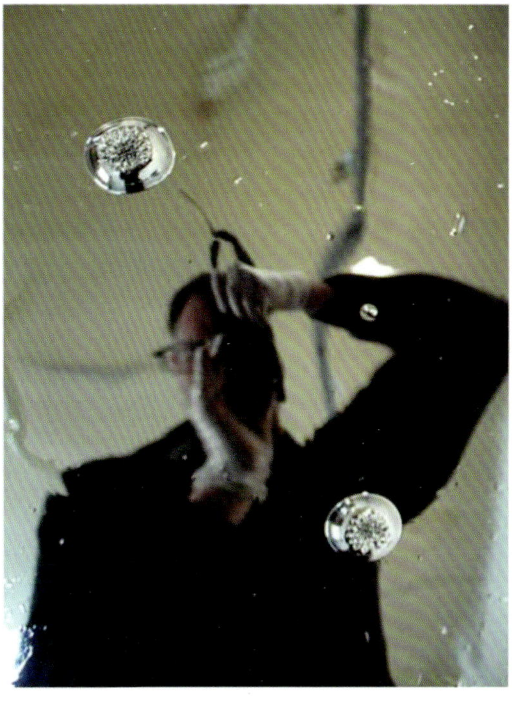

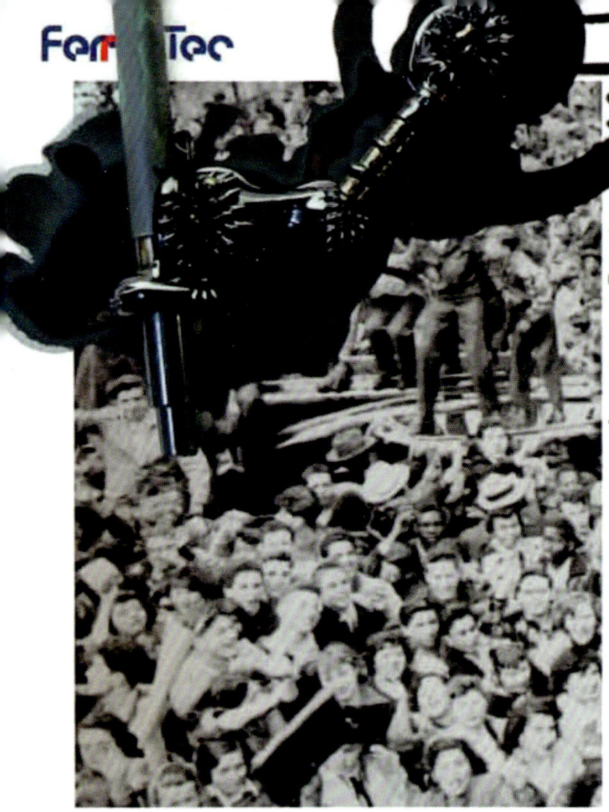

[redacted] industry [redacted] seals and vacuum rotary feedthroughs [redacted] quality [redacted] performance [redacted] seal [redacted] seals [redacted] demanding applications. [redacted] optimize [redacted] intense performance requirements.

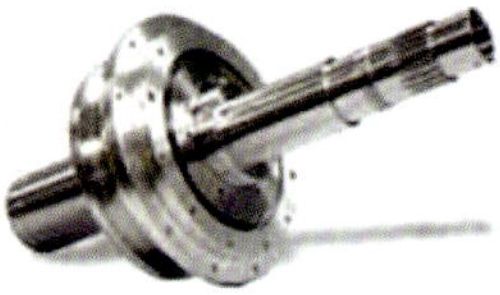

[redacted] produce [redacted] optimized [redacted] demands [redacted] target [redacted]cations. [redacted] competitive products [redacted] high-precision [redacted]

[redacted] feedthrough »
[redacted] seals and feedthroughs.

[redacted]

[redacted] stand-alone [redacted]

[redacted] engineer [redacted] performance requirements [redacted] target [redacted] precision, performance [redacted] reliability [redacted]

[redacted] vacuum feedthrough [redacted] repair [redacted] upgrade [redacted] solution. [redacted] service.

[redacted]

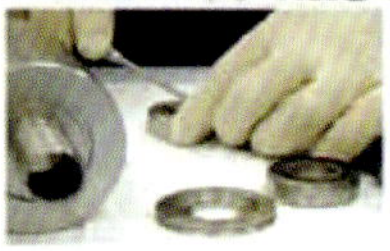

[redacted] existing [redacted] premium [redacted] product [redacted] optimized [redacted]

Learn more »

Seals for Airborne Electro-Optical Systems

Airborne electro-optics [redacted] infrared devices [redacted] surveillance cameras [redacted] ever-growing [redacted] military, law enforcement, [redacted] civilian activities.

[redacted]

- Target acquisition and designation
- Weapons guidance
- Forward-looking infrared (FLIR) devices
- Reconnaissance and surveillance

[redacted]

[redacted] electro-optical instruments [redacted] demanding airborne conditions. Hermetic seals [redacted] smooth, damped rotation [redacted] azimuth [redacted] elevation [redacted] constant pressure [redacted] optical pod. [redacted] integrate [redacted] bearing assemblies [redacted] customized interfaces [redacted] low-maintenance, highly integrated sealed gimbal systems [redacted] unlimited [redacted] diameters and sizes. Extremely low, consistent drag torque [redacted] servomotor power. [redacted] airborne enclosures [redacted] superior dynamic sealing [redacted] critical [redacted] optimum optical performance.

[redacted]

- True hermetic sealing
- High reliability
- Zero maintenance
- Low drag torque
- Wide thermal range
- Smooth operation
- Flexible configurations
- Compliance to military specifications and standards

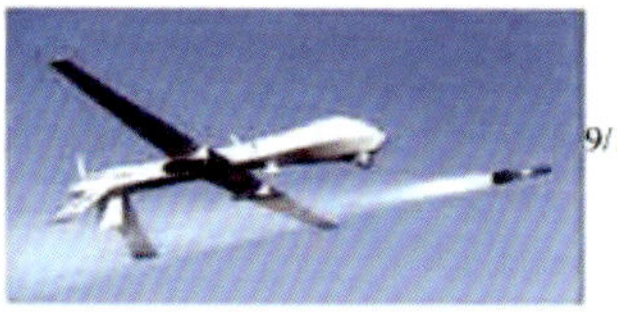

9/1/11 10:

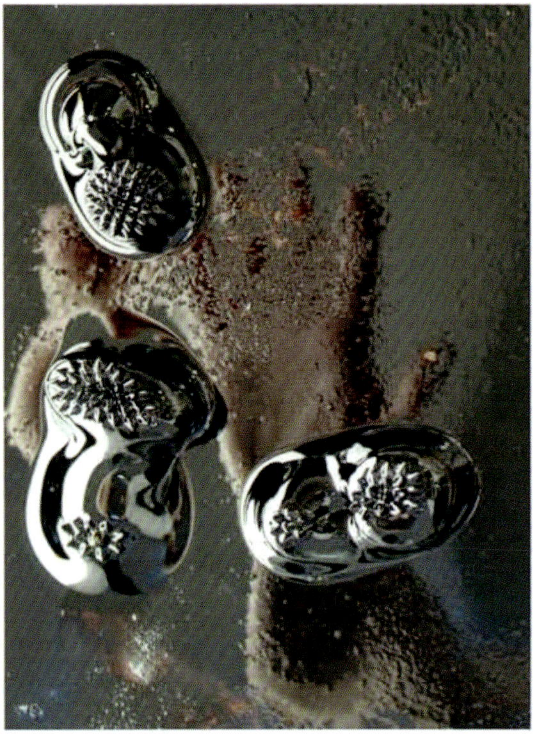

Leak-Free [redacted]

[redacted] movable camera pods [redacted] single axis and gimbaled multiple axis. [redacted] sealed interior chamber [redacted] moisture-free gas. [redacted] system must maintain [redacted] internal environment [redacted] subjected to dust, rain, aircraft fuels, de-icing spray and normal maintenance fluids, [redacted] outside temperatures and altitudes.

[redacted] hermetic sealing [redacted] smooth, low-power rotation. [redacted] elastomer lip seals [redacted] mechanical seals [redacted]. Retrofitting [redacted] equipment operation.

Gimbal Style Optical Pods (multiple axis)

Multiple axis scanning pods [redacted] smooth optical tracking [redacted] azimuth [redacted] elevation. [redacted] under-wing [redacted] in the nose [redacted] forward-looking [redacted] applications [redacted] extremely low drag torque [redacted] temperature range.

Single Axis Optical Tracking Systems

[redacted] under [redacted] wing [redacted] lower fuselage surface [redacted] scan [redacted] single axis [redacted] target. [redacted] optical pod [redacted] interfaces [redacted] stationary mounting bracket. [redacted] internal passage [redacted] cables, pressurization [redacted] optical path. [redacted] radial section, [redacted] precision ball [redacted] rotating [redacted] low-drag sealing [redacted] pressures exceeding one bar (14.5 psi).

[redacted] leak-free [redacted] higher pressure capability [redacted], exotic lightweight [redacted] heating [redacted] cooling [redacted] feedback [redacted]

Audio [redacted]

[redacted] global leader [redacted] audio speaker [redacted] speakers [redacted] function [redacted] efficiently, [redacted] audio response [redacted] power [redacted] manufacturability [redacted] quality and higher [redacted] yields.

[redacted] synthetic hydrocarbons [redacted] esters [redacted] oils [redacted] volatility [redacted] stability. [redacted] dictated [redacted] environmental [redacted] application

FerroTec

[redacted] magnetic tapes, rigid [redacted] floppy disks, magneto-optical disks, crystalline and amorphous alloys, garnets, steels and geological rocks.

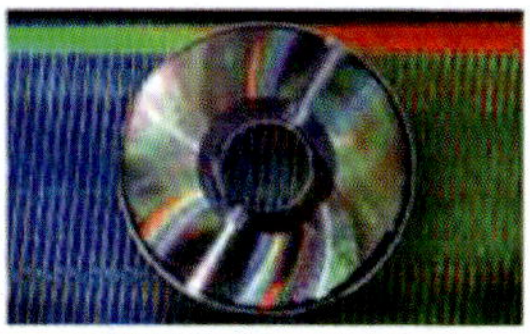

Commercial [redacted] control [redacted] recording media [redacted] identification [redacted] micro-defects [redacted] steel.

[redacted] magnetic tape, disk [redacted] specimen [redacted] surface [redacted] carrier liquid evaporates [redacted] particles congregate [redacted] boundaries. [redacted] dark lines [redacted] visible light [redacted] microscope [redacted] magnetic field [redacted] specimen [redacted] contrast [redacted] pattern.

[redacted] water [redacted] mineral oil [redacted] Domain detection [redacted] wetting agent [redacted] solvent [redacted]

[redacted] audio and video tape manufacturers, TV a[redacted]cording studios, forensic science laboratories [redacted] research institutions. A[redacted]ater-based a[redacted]

[redacted] Educational [redacted]

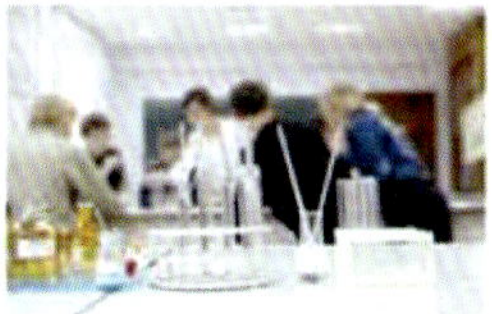

[redacted] amazing [redacted] visually [redacted], exciting [redacted] tool. [redacted] mind, [redacted] markets.

[redacted] maximize [redacted] environments, [redacted]xception. [redacted] visualize [redacted] magnetic patterns. Technical data [redacted]

[redacted] Adventure [redacted] patterns [redacted] thought [redacted] supervision.

Bio-Medical [redacted]

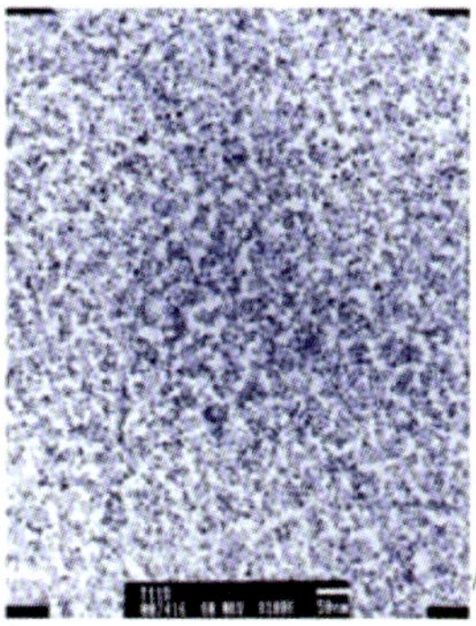

[redacted] diagnostic tests [redacted] malignant masses [redacted] an assortment of [redacted] lesions) [redacted] nanoparticles [redacted] materials [redacted] monomer [redacted] magnetic plastic) [redacted] polymer [redacted] shaped [redacted] other [redacted] micro-beads [redacted] bio-active materials. [redacted] beads [redacted] micro-spheres, [redacted] antibodies, DNA [redacted] diagnostic process (immunoassay [redacted] molecular diagnostics - separation and amplification). [redacted] coat [redacted] treat [redacted]

[redacted] site-specific delivery [redacted] hyperthermia [redacted] injected [redacted] biological system, [redacted] electromagnets [redacted] tumor [redacted] lesion. [redacted] infiltrate [redacted] gradient, [redacted] interstitial pressure [redacted] intravenous drug delivery. [redacted] strong excitation of [redacted] particles. [redacted] heat, [redacted] lesion, [redacted] killing [redacted] tissues. [redacted] drug coated material.

[redacted] in-vivo human testing [redacted] therapeutic applications. [redacted]

[redacted] bead manufacturers [redacted] research scientists - [redacted]ry particles [redacted] performance characteristics [redacted] optimized [redacted]

[redacted] particle distribution. [redacted] agglomerates [redacted] consistent performance [redacted] configurations, [redacted] (10 nm nominal) [redacted] more information.

[redacted] Applications

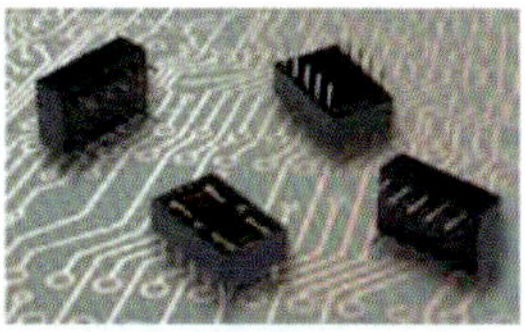

[redacted] R&D [redacted] strategic partnerships [redacted] material recycling, power and distribution transformers, quiet solenoids, sensors and switches.

Material Separation [redacted] Recycling

[redacted] apparent density [redacted] physical characteristic [redacted] separate objects [redacted] different density [redacted] floatation [redacted] sinking [redacted] mining industries, [redacted] economic advantage [redacted] commercialize [redacted] application [redacted] economic viability [redacted] patent-pending [redacted] reclamation [redacted] reconstitution [redacted] separation [redacted] materials.

Electrical Transformers

[redacted] electrical power equipment, [redacted] liquid-filled [redacted] thermal and dielectric [redacted]

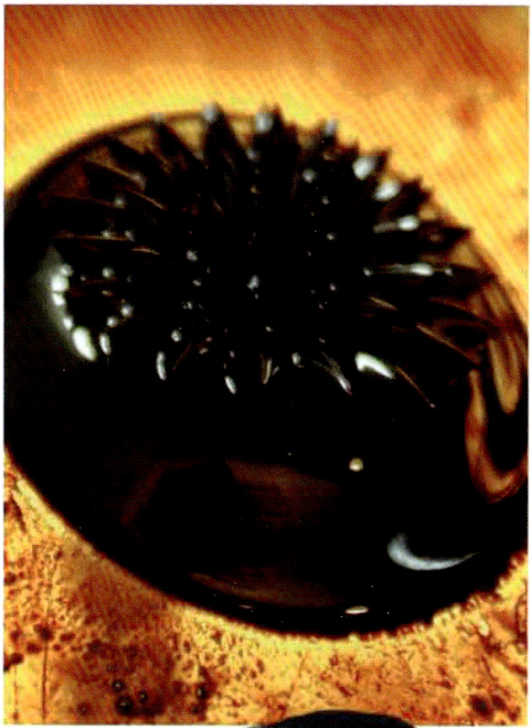

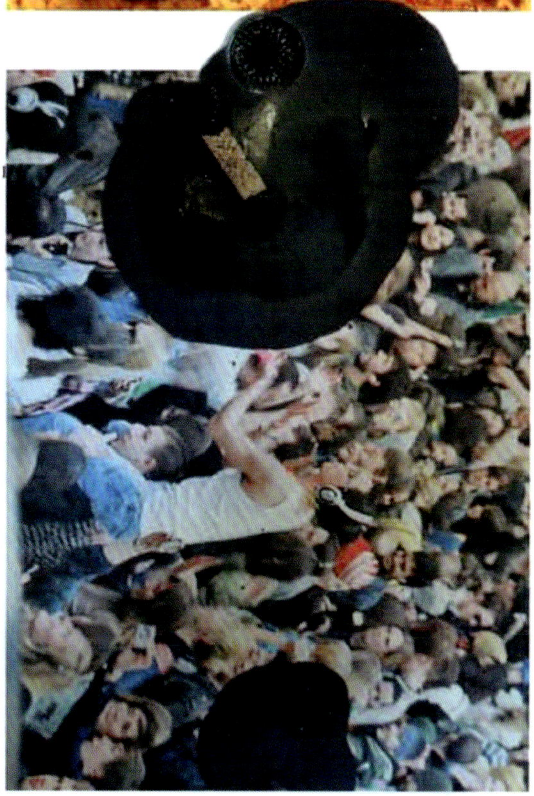

A Network of List of Good Jobs Skills, Jobs in Demand, Highest Paying Careers in 2011, Freelance Jobs Higher Sites

Home Backlinks List Of Job Skills Privacy Policy

Search this website...

15 Freelance Job Sites

ne 12, 2011 by admin · Leave a Comment
d under: 15 Freelance Job Sites

Share/Bookmark

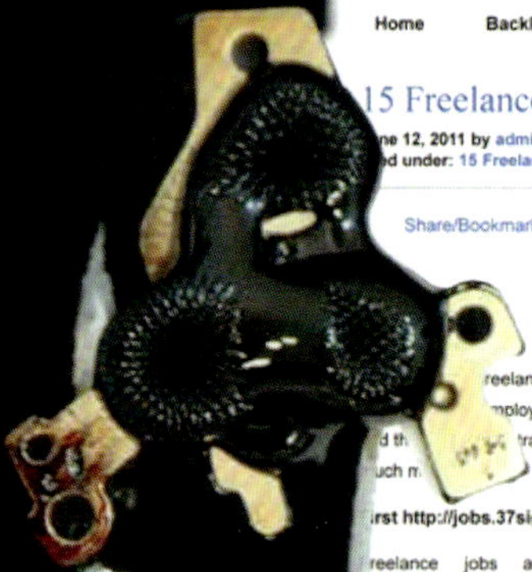

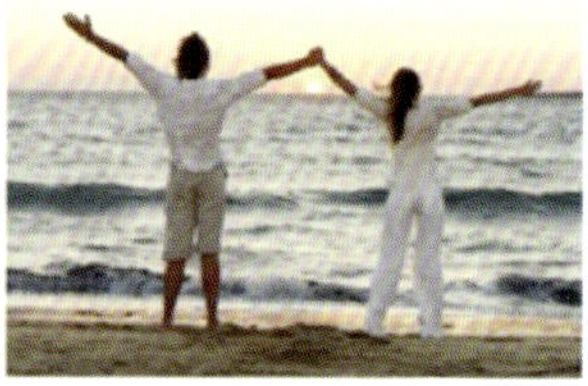

reelancing sites and
mployment, pages,
d th tract prices, and
uch m

irst http://jobs.37signals.com

reelance jobs are technical ignals Forum 37. 9-5 regular jobs sted here and make sure that the sts of independent research.

2nd http://www.artypapers.com

a list of the best sites on ... find some simple tips

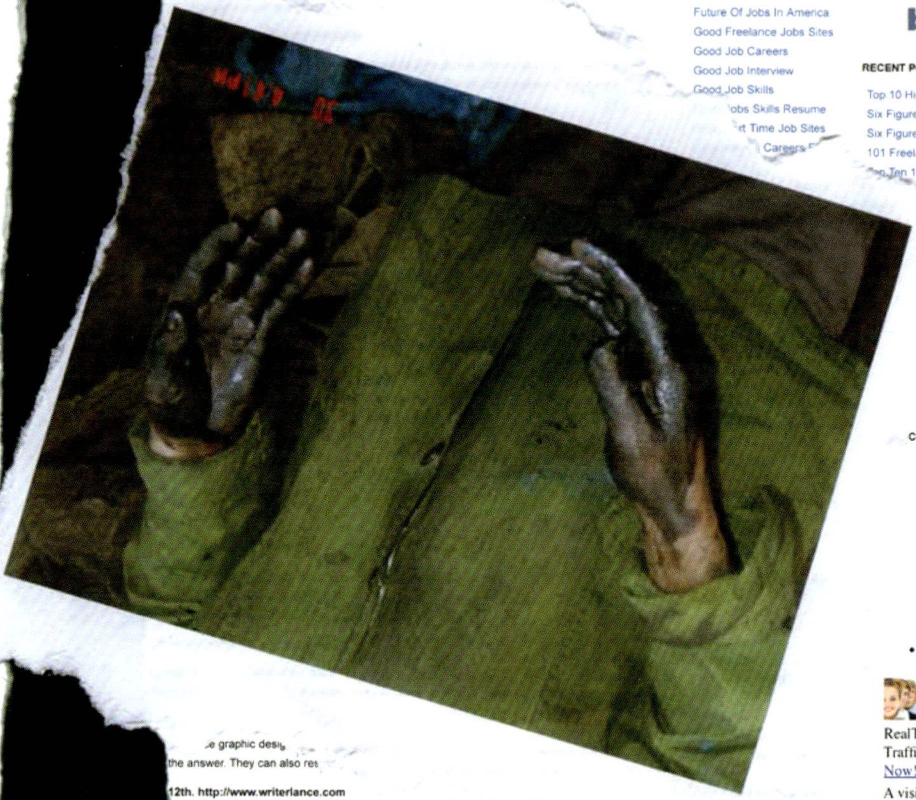

e graphic desi...
the answer. They can also re...

12th. http://www.writerlance.com

This site matches buyers with freelancers. There is no charge for this se... ontract requires a payment of $ 3 or 3%, which is the largest.

3th http://www.freelancefree.com

dependent, not a free professional guidance easier and more attractive. You can get a good b of different professions are looking for something a little different.

4th http://freelance.geekinterview.com

is is the place to find a job, regardless of income.

5th http://www.teamprojectsonly.com

e project team has been specially designed for independent developers. Technical writers d graphic designers can sometimes be able to find some good tracks here too.

gs: 15 Freelance Job Sites, Collection of Freelance Job Sites, Freelance Job Sites 2011, eelance Jobs, List of Freelance Job Sites

CATEGORIES

- 10 Best Paid Jobs
- 100K Career Opportunities
- 100k Salary Jobs
- 101 Freelance Job Sites
- 15 Freelance Job Sites
- 20 Freelance Job Websites
- 5 Places to Find Freelance Jobs
- 65 Best Freelance Job Sites
- Best Career Choice 2011
- Best Careers For 2011
- Best Careers For Women
- Best Paying Jobs Without A Degree
- Best Weekend Jobs
- Dangerous Careers
- Dangerous Jobs List
- Dangerous Jobs that Pay Well
- Future Of Jobs In America
- Good Freelance Jobs Sites
- Good Job Careers
- Good Job Interview
- Good Job Skills
- obs Skills Resume
- t Time Job Sites
- Careers
- Good Search Sites
- Lucrative Part Time Jobs
- Most Stressful Jobs in America
- Odd Jobs That Pay Well
- Online Jobs for Teens
- Part Time High Paying Jobs
- Part Time Jobs for Moms
- Part time Jobs For Students
- Part Time Jobs for Teens

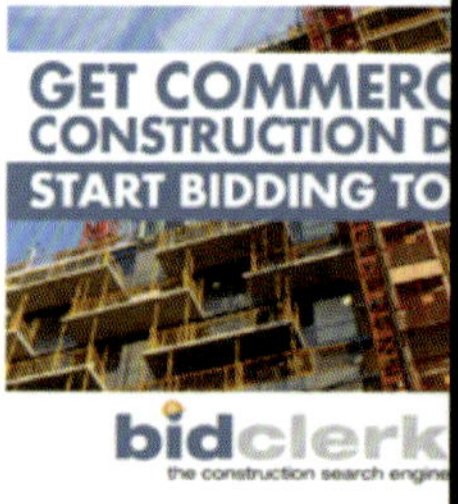

RECENT POSTS

- Top 10 High Paying Jobs for 2011
- Six Figure Jobs with a Bachelor's Degre
- Six Figure Jobs without Degree
- 101 Freelance Job Sites
- Top Ten 10 Dangerous Jobs that Pay We

TRACE

CONTROLER

- Live Traffic Feed

See your visitors in RealTime! Get the Free Live Traffic Feed Get Feedjit Now!

A visitor from Brooklyn, New York viewed "15 Freelance Job Sites | Good Job Skills" 0 secs ago

A visitor from Austin, Texas arrived 6 mins ago

A visitor from Denver, Colorado viewed "Top 5 Places to Find Freelance Jobs | Good Job Skills" 8 mins ago

A visitor from Macedonia viewed "Useful List of Freelance Job Sites | Good Job Skills" 9 mins ago

A visitor from Jakarta, Jakarta Raya viewed "20

Index of works:

Sam Lewitt
Fluid Employment

Editor: Sam Lewitt
Copy Editor: Daniel Berchenko
Design: Joseph Logan & Sam Lewitt,
assisted by Rachel Hudson

Photo Credits: Sam Lewitt, Nick Ash (Galerie Buchholz), Jeffrey Sturges (Miguel Abreu Gallery)

Published by:

Koenig Books Ltd
At the Serpentine Gallery
Kensington Gardens
London W2 3XA
www.koenigbooks.co.uk

Galerie Buchholz

Neven-DuMont-Str. 17, 50667 Köln
Tel: +49 (0)221 257 49 46

Fasanenstr. 30, 10719 Berlin
Tel: +49 (0)30 88 62 40 56

post@galeriebuchholz.de
www.galeriebuchholz.de

Sequence Press
36 Orchard Street, New York, NY 10002
www.sequencepress.com

Bibliographic information published by the Deutsche Nationalbibliothek.
The Deutsche Nationalbibliothek lists this publication in the Deutsche Nationalbibliografie; detailed bibliographic data are available in the Internet at http://dnb.d-nb.de.

Printed and bound in Italy by Conti Tipocolor S.p.A

Distribution:

Buchhandlung Walther König
Ehrenstr. 4, 50672 Köln
Tel. +49 (0) 221 / 20 59 6-53
Fax +49 (0) 221 / 20 59 6-60
verlag@buchhandlung-walther-koenig.de

Switzerland: AVA Verlagsauslieferungen AG
Centralweg16
CH-8910 Affoltern a.A.
Tel. +41 (44) 762 42 60
Fax +41 (44) 762 42 10
verlagsservice@ava.ch

UK & Eire: Cornerhouse Publications
70 Oxford Street, GB-Manchester M1 5NH
Tel. +44 (0) 161 200 15 03
Fax +44 (0) 161 200 15 04
publications@cornerhouse.org

Outside Europe: Sequence Press
36 Orchard Street, New York, NY 10002
Tel. +1 212 995 1774
Fax +1 646 688 2302
post@sequencepress.com

ISBN 978-3-86335-315-5

Acknowledgments:

A special note of gratitude to Elisabeth Sussman and Jay Sanders for providing the initial opportunity and support for the realization of *Fluid Employment*.

The artist would also like to thank the following for their direct involvement:

Miguel Abreu, Daniel Berchenko, Richard Birkett, Nathan Brown, Daniel Buchholz, Greta Hartenstein, Stefan Kalmár, Alex Kitnick, Joseph Logan, Dana Miller, Christopher Müller, Katherine Pickard, Elisabeth Sherman, Esme Watanabe

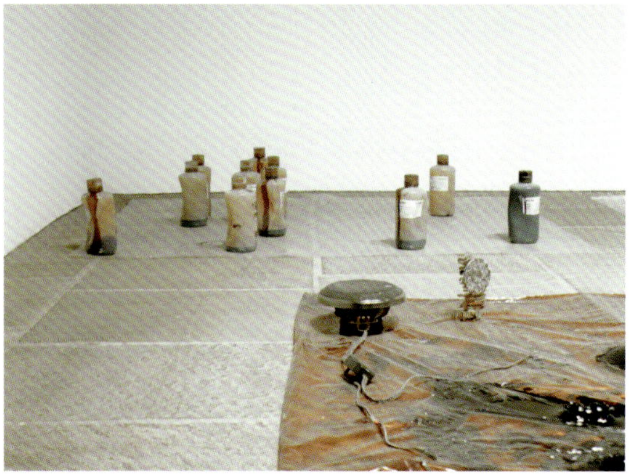

For R.A.W. and the unknown one